The Disinherited

Nadar's photograph of Nerval aged about thirty-six
Photo George Sirot

The Disinherited

THE LIFE OF
GÉRARD DE NERVAL
1808–1855

Benn Sowerby

PETER OWEN · LONDON

ISBN 0 7206 0083 0

To Lorna

PETER OWEN LIMITED
20 Holland Park Avenue London W11 3QU

First British Commonwealth edition 1973
© 1973 Benn Sowerby

Printed in Great Britain by
Bristol Typesetting Co Ltd
Barton Manor Bristol 2

Contents

Illustrations

The Disinherited

I am the wanderer, widowed and desolate,
Prince of Aquitaine, of the ruined towers.
My one star is lost; on my lute predestinate
The black sun of Melancholy grimly lours.

In this night of the tomb, dear friend so compassionate,
Bring me Pausilippo again, and the sea, and that flower
That eased my heart once of its grievous weight,
And the trellis the rose and the vine embower.

Am I Eros or Phoebus? . . . Lusignan or Biron?
Where a queen's lips touched my brow the bright seal never dims.
I have dreamed in grottoes where the Siren swims.

And twice now, triumphant, I have crossed Acheron;
On Orpheus's lyre alternating my lay
To the sigh of the saint and the call of the fay.

Gérard de Nerval

Introduction

In the winter of 1854-5 the Paris quarter of the Old Butcheries was undoubtedly the most squalid corner of the city. Known then as the 'Vale of Misery', it was a maze of narrow streets just east of the Place du Châtelet. One of these, the Rue de la Tuerie, led between blank walls to an obscure and evil-smelling alley. Here a great lantern, hanging above a door which was reached by a wooden balcony at street level, indicated the entrance to a shabby lodging-house. Beside the balcony a flight of seven stone steps descended to a landing protected by a rusty iron railing, on which during the daytime a sinister-looking raven would stalk sedately up and down, periodically uttering the only words it could repeat, 'J'ai soif' (I'm thirsty). A second flight of five steps continued obliquely beneath the balcony to emerge in the alley below, the Rue de la Vieille Lanterne, its broken paving deep in mud and filth. Just beyond the foot of the steps there was a grille in the wall and a second door to the lodging-house. A low vaulted passage on the opposite side leading directly to the Seine served as an open drain for the neighbouring houses. It was here, after a night of bitter cold, that the body of Gérard de Nerval was found on the morning of 26 January 1855, hanging from the grille at the bottom of the steps. It was a tragic and sordid end to a life which has fascinated biographers and which still invites fresh interpretation.

Despite the autobiographical nature of a great part of Nerval's writing, it is clear that fact and fiction, reminiscence and reverie, imagination and hallucination are purposely confounded, and there is perhaps a temptation to interpret the myth of his tragic destiny too literally. Nevertheless, that destiny would seem to be clearly traced throughout his life in the vain search for an impossible ideal of feminine beauty which had its source in the loss of his mother and his traumatic encounter as a child with the young girl Adrienne, and which finally helped to destroy him.

It is perhaps not surprising that Nerval's best work was under-rated by his contemporaries. For them he was, in Barrès' phrase, 'the delightful madman'. They were charmed by him but they never took him completely seriously. His persistent but misapplied efforts to make a name for himself as a dramatist brought him disappointment and disillusion and perhaps helped to obscure his real achievement. But he had a surprisingly modern sensibility, and time has procured him recognition, at least in his own country. Nerval's modesty was such that he would doubtless have been amazed at the number of posthumous editions of his works and the variety of critical studies that have continued to appear ever since the publication of Aristide Marie's biography in 1914. Baudelaire, it is true, paid tribute to his 'brilliant, active and luminous intellect' and more than fifty years after his death Apollinaire wrote of his 'charming spirit! I should have loved him like a brother'; but it was Proust who, acknowledging his debt to Nerval, first recognized his genius. 'He is', said Proust, 'assuredly one of the three or four greatest writers of the nineteenth century.' Later, the Surrealists acclaimed him and paved the way for a serious study of his life and work by a host of biographers and critics, so that today Nerval's position in the history of French literature is firmly established.

1

Early Days

Although the pseudonym 'de Nerval' is generally and justly associated with the Valois country in the Ile de France, Gérard Labrunie was born in Paris and spent the greater part of his life there. Nevertheless he did not consider himself a true Parisian. 'I am very fond of Paris,' he wrote, 'where, as chance would have it, I was born, but I might just as well have been born on a ship. . . . A man from the South, merely because he happens to get married there to a woman from the North, cannot produce a child with a really Parisian nature.' There can be little doubt that the fantastic genealogy he invented for himself was in part an attempt to overcome a feeling of rootlessness. He was by nature a nomad, and his story is that of a wanderer between country and country, and between dream and reality, until that dream became progressively more real to him than the nightmare of his life.

The 'man from the South' was Etienne Labrunie, born at Agen in 1776 of a humble family of artisans. Gérard hypothetically traced his father's family back to the three lords Brunyer de la Brunie, knights at the court of Otho the Great, one of whom settled in Périgord on the banks of the Dordogne. When he was barely sixteen Etienne Labrunie left his family to join the army. Wounded twice by the age of nineteen and discharged with a small pension, he went to Paris to study medicine. After ten years' determined application, for he had no educational background, he gained his degree in 1806. Two years later he was granted a commission as a medical officer to the Grande Armée at the age of thirty-two.

Meanwhile he had met Marie Antoinette Laurent, a linen-draper's daughter, and they were married on 1 July 1807. She was the 'woman of the North'. Gérard relates how, as a young man, Marie's father, Pierre Charles Laurent, left his native village of Laffaux, between Soissons and Laon, after a violent argument with his father. He settled at the little village of Mortefontaine where a distant relative, Adrien Boucher, kept an inn. He went into service with the Le Peletier family in Mortefontaine and subsequently moved with them to Paris, where he later set up in business as a linen-draper. After Adrien Boucher's death, Pierre Charles returned to marry the old man's daughter, Marie Marguerite Victoire, a circumstance in which some commentators have seen the genesis of Gérard's madness. (In Gérard's account they were first cousins.)

Of their three children, Pierre Louis died at birth, while Marie Antoinette Marguerite (Gérard's mother, born in 1785) and Eugénie (Gérard's aunt and only eight years older than himself) both died at the early age of twenty-five.

Marie Antoinette Marguerite was twenty-two when she married Etienne Labrunie. The young couple lived in an apartment near his uncle Dublanc in the Rue St Martin, and it was there that Gérard was born on 22 May 1808. He was baptized on 23 May in the church of St Merry and almost immediately put out to nurse with a peasant woman at Loisy, a tiny village close to Mortefontaine.

On 22 December Etienne Labrunie was called up to join the army of the Rhine. The decision to leave her seven-months-old child must have been a bitter one for Marie, but she felt that her duty lay with her husband and she resolved to follow him. During the Austrian campaign she accompanied him to Aukstam, to Danzig and to Linz. On 7 April 1810 they returned to Germany, where Dr Labrunie was in charge of the hospital in Hanover until 6 June, when he was transferred to Glogau. For a year and a half the young mother, deprived of her child, endured the rigours of war alongside her zealous and overworked husband, who can have had little time to devote to her needs. Finally she contracted a fever from which she died on 29 November 1810. She was buried, as Gérard tells us, 'in cold Silesia, in the Catholic cemetery of Gross-Glogau'. He adds, 'My father, forced to rejoin the army in Moscow, later lost her letters and jewellery in the waves of the Beresina.' It was not until the autumn of 1813 that news was received at home that Dr Labrunie had been taken prisoner near Smolensk, and, later, after the terrible crossing of the Beresina, had been seriously wounded on entering Vilna.

'I never saw my mother,' Gérard continues. 'Her portraits were either lost or stolen. I only know that she resembled a contemporary engraving, after Prudhon or Fragonard, which was called "Modesty". The fever of which she died has overtaken me three times at regular periodic intervals in my life. Always at these times my mind has been afflicted with the images of gloom and desolation that surrounded my cradle. The letters which my mother wrote from the shores of the Baltic or the banks of the Spree or the Danube, were read to me so many times! A sense of the marvellous and a taste for distant travels were no doubt in my case the result of these early impressions, as also of my long sojourn in a countryside isolated in the midst of woods.'

It was this country of mists, of lakes and meandering streams, of deep, shadowy forests – Chantilly, Ermenonville, Hallate, Compiègne – that Gérard was later to make peculiarly his own. When he was two years old he was taken from Loisy and since his grandparents were too occupied with their Paris business to look after him, he went to live with his great-uncle, Antoine Boucher. This man kept a little grocery shop in what had formerly been the inn at Mortefontaine where, years before, Adrien Boucher had welcomed his young runaway relative from beyond Soissons.

Gérard grew to love his great-uncle who, in those early years, took the place of his absent father. He describes him as a 'man who was good all his life with a slight tendency to misanthropy with which I gently reproached him'. In his simple way Antoine Boucher directed the child's first steps in education. He had made a hobby of collecting Roman and Celtic remains. The house in which he lived occupied the site of an ancient Roman camp. The land, about two acres, was known as the 'clos de Nerva' or 'clos de Nerval', being named after the last of the Roman emperors, and it was from this 'field of Nerval' that Gérard later derived his pseudonym. Sometimes, digging here, Antoine would turn up ancient coins, medals and pots, and Gérard tells us that he had 'found on his land or in the neighbourhood images of gods and emperors which his admiration as a connoisseur caused me to regard with veneration'. There were other carved figures, too, a Neptune and an Amphitrite over a fountain, besides the Christian effigies in the church, which also had 'two misshapen saints at the entrance'. The young Gérard was naturally bewildered by these different symbols. One day he asked his great-uncle, 'What is God?' 'God is the sun,' was the reply. 'It was', he says, 'the inmost thought of a good man who had been a Christian all his life, but who had lived through the Revolution, and who belonged to a part of the country in which many shared this same idea of the Divinity.' Nevertheless the women and children attended church regularly, and it was one of his aunts, no doubt Eugénie, whom he loved, who first taught him to appreciate something of the principles of the Christian faith. When he was a little older he was introduced to the Sermon on the Mount and given a New Testament. No doubt the confusion of these various ideas contributed, as he himself suggests, to his ambivalent attitude towards religion in later life.

Clearly Antoine Boucher's house was a real home to Gérard. Returning to it some years after his uncle's death, he was filled with sadness at the sight of its yellow exterior with the green shutters, unchanged since his childhood, and he lingered lovingly over the old furniture which had not yet been moved and was still kept dusted and polished. There were two paintings, supposedly by a Flemish ancestor, prints after Boucher and engravings by Moreau. The latter were illustrations of the works of Rousseau, who had lived in this region for a short while before his death at nearby Ermenonville, and who was to exercise a profound influence on Gérard throughout his life. A collection of Roman remains found in the garden still lay on the desk in the study and there was a book-case filled with his uncle's favourite books.

Of his uncle's library Gérard gives a rather exaggerated account. He tells of the books he discovered piled up and forgotten in the attic, gnawed by rats, damp and mouldy from the rain seeping through the cracks between the tiles. These, he says, were of a mystical and cabbalistic nature and had been relegated there when his uncle had adopted a modified form of deism. In the neighbourhood of Ermenonville, the meeting-place of such men as Count St Germain, Mesmer, Cagliostro and later Sénancour and Cazotte among others, some works of this kind might well be found. We know that at Mortefontaine Gérard first read the Abbé de Villars, d'Argens, and Dom Pernety, the translator of Swedenborg. There was plenty here to fill an immature mind with a variety of extravagant mystical notions. 'At an early age', he says, 'my mind absorbed a great deal of this indigestible and unhealthy nourishment'; and it proved to be a lasting influence.

But the hours spent poring over those tattered old volumes in the attic occurred later when he returned to Mortefontaine during his holidays from school. For the present his time was largely spent in exploring the countryside, sometimes with his uncle Antoine and the dog, but more often further afield among the villages of Charlepont, Pontarmé, Thiers, Châalis, Ver, Otys, Orry, Bertranfosse, with children of his own age or a little older, mostly girls. Just as his great-uncle took the place of his absent father, so these young girls took the place of his dead mother. There were many of them, and they mingle and interchange in his work just as they must have done for him in real life : Sophie, Emerance, Sidonie, Sylvie, Célénie, Delphine, Héloise. With Célénie he would gather flowers on the banks of the Comelle ponds; she loved the grottoes hidden in the woods, the ruins of old chateaux, and the crumbled temples with ivy-covered columns. Then there was Sylvie, rather wild, with bare feet and sunburned skin, shouting with delight as she darted here and there among the rocks and dolmens. Sometimes they wandered together along the banks of the Nonette; it was Sylvie who taught him to catch shrimps under the bridges of the Nonette and the Thève, and perhaps she who one day saved him from drowning. He had fallen into deep water and was clutching desperately at the iris leaves which tore his hands when she flung herself down on her stomach and pulled him out by the hair with all her strength.

There was singing and dancing, too. Gérard gives us the picture of Emerance sitting on a low stone wall by the well in the square, singing to a troupe of smaller girls, organizing their choruses and joining in their dance. Stories were told by the fireside and Gérard grew to love the old songs and legends of the Valois. The dancing ground, with its benches for the old people to sit and watch, was then in regular use. And there were festivals, when the young girls came dressed in white to receive their prizes for study and good behaviour at the Temple of Philosophy at Ermenonville, now a ruin overgrown with ivy and brambles. But above all there were the archery festivals announced by horn and drum echoing through the woods. The young girls sang as they sat weaving garlands and arranging bouquets tied with gay ribbons which were heaped on to a lumbering ox waggon as it passed, followed by the procession of self-titled knights with their bows and arrows, Gérard among them. Such were the simple pleasures upon which, after all his wanderings, he came to look back with deep nostalgia.

He was seven years old when, as he was playing outside his uncle's door one day, three officers came up to the house. One of them picked him up and embraced him so strongly that he cried out spontaneously, 'Father! . . . You're hurting me.' It was indeed Dr Etienne Labrunie, returned from Russia, disabled and discharged, after having been 'saved from the waves of the icy Beresina'. 'From that day', says Gérard, 'my destiny was changed.'

One is scarcely surprised to detect in this a note of protest. Gérard had never known his mother. It seemed to him almost as if there had been a conspiracy of fate to deprive him of her, and it is surely significant that he says 'her portraits were either lost or *stolen*'. Until now the kindly figure of his uncle Antoine had been a sufficient substitute for his father but not even the older girls among his playfellows had been able to compensate him for the loss of his mother's care and affection. Now the sudden appearance of Dr Labrunie with his clumsy if heartfelt greeting must have seemed like that of a usurper. Moreover, it helped to bring home to Gérard that he would never know his mother. He may well have seen this stern-looking stranger as in some way responsible for her death. It was a crisis that had a lasting effect upon their relationship. That Dr Labrunie was a generally undemonstrative man is without question. The harsh experiences of army life from the age of sixteen onwards had roughened him, but he was not without feeling. That the death of his wife was a severe blow to him is shown by a brief passage in which Gérard recalls that as a young man, newly returned from Poland, his father sang Italian airs with some taste, 'and, as he accompanied himself on the guitar, could not help crying at the words of a song which she had loved.'

A new and very different life now began for Gérard. Dr Labrunie took him away to live in Paris in the Rue St Martin. The strict régime to which he was subjected in this somewhat comfortless household was in strong contrast with his carefree existence at Mortefontaine. Before dawn he would be awakened by his father's batman, and together they would walk over the hills around Paris, the young Gérard often trotting to keep pace with the military stride of his companion. Before returning they would breakfast on bread and cream at a farm or dairy. The rest of the day was devoted to lessons.

Gérard was at the time, he himself says, rather backward, but the determination and strict discipline of his father was soon to rectify this. There was to be no relaxation, and only the gaiety and cheerfulness of the doctor's younger brother, one of the three officers who had arrived at Mortefontaine that sunny morning, mitigated the austerity and eased the burden of work. The formidable list of subjects to be studied grew over the next few years. Gérard applied himself diligently. 'My handwriting,' he says with modest pride, 'carefully cultivated, at times rivalled in grace and correctness that of the most famous manuscripts of Iran.' He attended dancing-school and studied music and drawing. He early developed a love of the classics and also studied other languages. Dr Labrunie had set up a small practice to supplement his pension, but he found time to teach his son German, which he thought would be particularly useful to Gérard in the diplomatic career he planned for him. At the same time, Gérard studied Italian, Arabic and Persian. However, it is clear that his knowledge remained superficial, since he later wrote to Houssaye, 'I confess to you, my friend, that although I know a number of languages I have a very imperfect knowledge of them. As I learned them chiefly from books and newspapers the *accent* defeats me, intimidates me, prevents me from recognizing the words.' Nevertheless he was clearly a willing pupil and made rapid progress.

Of this period of his life Gérard tells us very little. He mentions one incident, however, which throws some light on his disposition. He had been given a turtledove of which he was very fond. 'One day,' he relates, 'one of the fine ladies who visited my father asked some slight service of me : as ill luck would have it, I answered her impatiently. When I returned to the terrace, the turtledove had flown away. I was so grieved at this that I almost died of a purpuric fever, which drove all the blood from my heart to my skin. They thought to console me by giving me for companion a young monkey, brought back from America by a captain, a friend of my father's. This pretty animal became my constant companion at play and at work.' The gentle Gérard could, then, occasionally revolt, but the succeeding sense of guilt, even more than the loss of his pet, brought on a nervous fever so severe that he almost succumbed to it.

At that time he was a good-looking child, with rather pale cheeks, grey eyes and wavy fair hair which fell capriciously over a high forehead. Always docile, sensitive and amenable, his natural exuberance was of necessity subdued in the company of the retired army doctor who had no great capacity for sympathy and did not encourage confidences from others.

When he was twelve Gérard entered Charlemagne Grammar School as a day pupil and it was here that he met Théophile Gautier, with whom he formed a close and lifelong friendship. He worked hard and was an exemplary pupil, always near the top of his class. He took the prize for Latin verse and in 1826 competed for the Académie française prize for rhetoric. The subject for that year was the literature of the sixteenth century. His essay did not win the prize which was shared by two men considerably older than himself. Stung by this disappointment Gérard gave vent to his feelings in satire. He had been writing verse since the age of thirteen, but as yet showed no sign of developing into the poet of *Les Chimères*. Although he was to become a staunch supporter of the Romantic Movement, his veneration for the classics led him in this early satire into a virulent criticism of the romantic style which he saw as 'piling up big words, always devoid of meaning', and he adjured his school-fellow Duponchet to 'shun those dazzling verses in which everything is for show regardless of content.' In the same year he published his *Elégies Nationales*, political and patriotic poems inspired by youthful enthusiasm but pedestrian in style. They were, however, well received by his fellow students, among whom he was already earning something of a reputation. Gautier tells us that at this time he was a 'quiet and modest young man who blushed like a girl and was always ready to avoid the admiring curiosity of his school-fellows, proud indeed to have a comrade in print who was talked of in the papers.' Before he left college he had already been in print six times and had become a contributor to the *Mercure de France au XIXe Siècle* which was edited by Paul Lacroix, better known as the bibliophile Jacob, his friend and patron.

But it was the publication in 1827 of his translation in prose and verse of the first part of Goethe's *Faust* that first brought him public recognition. Years before, as a child, he had been fascinated by a copy of Klinger's *Faust* which he found in a second-hand bookshop. A picture of the tiny, helpless Faust held between the finger and thumb of an enormous fire-breathing devil had particularly enthralled him. He now returned to *Faust* with renewed enthusiasm. Two previous translations had appeared three years before, and it seems probable that he made use of Stapfer's uninspired but exact version to help out his own incomplete knowledge of German. Be that as it may, he succeeded at the age of nineteen in producing a translation of remarkable verve, which was immediately acclaimed. It won high praise from Goethe himself who said, 'I have never understood myself so well as in reading you.' Gérard, who was in deep sympathy with the work, had discovered something of himself in the character of Faust. He too 'experienced something of that predicament of the human spirit, which longs unceasingly for divine revelations, which stretches, so to speak, the whole length of its chain, until the moment when cold reality comes to disenchant the boldness of its illusions and hopes and . . . throws it back into the dusty world.' In his own way, he too was to seek 'in hell the help that heaven refused him'.

Eugène de Mirecourt relates the story of Goethe's reception of the work. One evening in 1827, after dinner with Eckermann, he was dipping into a book with evident delight. Eckermann asked him what he was reading and Goethe replied, 'I am reading a French translation of my *Faust*.'

'Ah yes,' said Eckermann with a touch of disdain. 'I have heard of it. It is by a young man of eighteen. I expect it smacks of the college.'

'Eighteen!' exclaimed Goethe. 'Well, mark me; this translation is a veritable prodigy of style. Its author will become one of the purest and most elegant writers in France.' And he added, 'I don't like *Faust* in German any more, but in this translation everything comes to life again with freshness and vivacity. I am filled with pride when I think that my book is made known in the language of Bossuet, Corneille and Racine. I repeat, this young man will go far.' Touquet, the publisher of some of Gérard's earliest works, had already told him : 'Young man, you will go far,' a prediction on which Gérard gaily commented later, 'Destiny has proved him right by inspiring me with a passion for long journeys.'

Another admirer of the book was Hector Berlioz. It made a profound impression on him and, as we learn from his *Mémoires*, he 'read it continually at table, in the theatre, in the streets, everywhere.' He even set some of the verses to music and these were later incorporated in his opera *La Damnation de Faust*.

The triumphant success of his translation opened new prospects for the young Gérard. Editors welcomed his contributions, both in verse and prose. Now, too, he began to move in literary and artistic circles. His friend, Théophile Gautier, who had begun by studying art before turning to literature, introduced him to various artists, among them Célestin Nanteuil. Chief of Gérard's young literary friends was Pétrus Borel, later to become known as 'Le Lycanthrope' (The Werewolf). Others, men mostly older than himself and already quite well known, such as Béranger, Thiers, Gavarni, Hugo, Dumas and Balzac, he probably met at Mother Saguet's tavern. Here, as Gérard tells in an article published in 1830, some twenty or so of them gathered regularly and were to be found drinking, singing and talking round the great central table with its three widely-spaced candles, its surface littered with tankards, cigars and a few hunks of cheese. 'Through all this trivial and frenzied tumult', he says, 'you will catch snatches of conversation something more than merely witty, bold and profound thoughts, and views on art developed with genius.' Gérard himself was a brilliant and charming talker and despite his timidity seems to have felt at home in such a milieu.

His interests were now largely centred in the literary life of Paris. All contacts with the idyllic life of his childhood had gradually been broken. His great-uncle, Antoine Boucher, whom he had visited regularly, died in 1820. Six years later his dearly-loved aunt Eugénie died. She had been his only real link with the mother whom he had never seen and whom he never ceased to regret. He was strangely impressed by the fact that both sisters died at the same early age. It seemed to him pre-ordained by a malicious fate. There were to be many such curious coincidences in his life, but it was perhaps this one that first induced him to look for a symbolic significance in them, and gave rise to what was to become a superstitious mania. Finally, the death of his grandmother, Marguerite Victoire Laurent, two years later in 1828 marked the extinction of his mother's line.

But although Gérard's connection with that already distant past was to all appearances completely severed, the old influences were secretly at work deep within him and were yet to develop and dominate his life.

2

Ideal Love

Returning in his maturity to 'that old country of Valois where, for more than a thousand years, has throbbed the heart of France', Gérard gathered up the reminiscences of his childhood. His evocation in *Sylvie* of the sights, scents and sounds of that countryside is vividly authentic, yet Gérard himself says, 'in recounting these details, I have to ask myself whether they are real or whether I have not perhaps dreamed them.' Certain incidents which recur in slightly different forms throughout his work reveal the strong impression they made upon him. There is, for example, his rescue from drowning in the Thève or Oise, already mentioned. There is the development and elaboration of a childish mock-marriage incident, first in a letter to Stadler in which he recounts how he and Sidonie dressed up in the wedding-clothes of her uncle and aunt at Saint Germain, then in *Promenades et Souvenirs,* where he gives a more detailed account of his mock-marriage with Fanchette, and finally in *Sylvie,* where he and Sylvie, on a visit to her aunt at Othys, steal upstairs to deck themselves out in the wedding-clothes they find preserved in a drawer; they startle the old woman with a momentary vision of herself and her dead husband on their wedding day; 'we were bridegroom and bride for a whole lovely summer morning' he concludes.

Whether or not the more extravagant episodes related really happened, the character of Sylvie is undoubtedly a composite of 'all those white phantoms of youth, whose breath revives a thousand dead thoughts.' The significance of Sylvie and of Adrienne (to whom we are introduced in *Sylvie,* although hints of such a figure had already appeared elsewhere) is clear : for Gérard the two figures represented 'two halves of a single love', of which he says, 'one was the sublime ideal, the other the sweet reality.' Adrienne appears as the central figure in a scene of great intensity, involving a young boy who is clearly Gérard himself. On the wide lawn before a château, surrounded by limes and elms, through the foliage of which the slanting rays of the setting sun pierce fierily, children are dancing – young girls, and among them one boy. The clear, pure voices of the girls accompany the round in an old song of the Valois country. Suddenly, in the regular course of the dance, the boy finds himself alone face to face with a tall fair-haired girl in the centre of the circle. He has scarcely noticed her until this moment, but now he is struck by her singular beauty. They are told to kiss each other, and, as the long ringlets of her golden hair brush his cheeks, he is overwhelmed by a bewildering emotion entirely new to him. Before she can rejoin the dance the girl must pay the forfeit of a song. The rest sit round her on the ground. As she sings, the shadows deepen under the tall elms, and the light of the rising moon falls on her alone, in the centre of the circle of attentive faces. The song ends. In the silence that follows, trailing vapours of white mist stealing over the lawn lend an ethereal enchantment to the scene. None dares to break the spell until suddenly the boy jumps up, runs to the terrace where there are laurels growing in great, coloured earthenware pots, and brings back two branches. These are twisted into a crown and tied with a ribbon. The boy takes it and places it upon her head in silent admiration. The tall, fair-haired girl rises, bows gracefully to her companions and runs back into the château. Adrienne was, Gérard tells us, a descendant of the Valois, and he goes on to say that she departed on the following day for a convent where she was a boarder, leaving him with the image of a 'vague, impossible love . . . a mirage of glory and beauty, sweetening the hours of harsh study.' The next year he learned that she had taken the veil at the convent of Saint Sulpice du Désert, where she died in 1832. He seems to have seen her once more taking part in a mystery play among the ruins of Châalis Abbey, where she represented a spirit ascending from the abyss with a flaming sword in her hand, her head encircled with a golden halo. A similar scene is presented in *Angélique* but this time it is a performance at Senlis : 'A very lovely blonde girl appeared in a white robe, with a head-dress of pearls and a halo and sword of gold, on a half-globe representing a burnt-out star. . . . She belonged to one of the greatest families of that part of the country and was called Delphine.'

There can be no doubt that some such encounter as that depicted in the moonlight setting of the lawn before the château actually took place and that the youthful Gérard experienced an overwhelming emotion that he never forgot, and which affected him all the more profoundly because he attempted to repress it. In his writings the scene is heightened and idealized. Names and places are changed and the story modified in various works.

Adrienne also is clearly a composite figure. She recalls the Emerance who appears in an earlier fragment, singing to the younger children at Senlis, and also the clever and vivacious Louise of the *Promenades et Souvenirs,* who took part in the young people's performances. The latter has been identified as Louise Céline de Junquière, who was born at the château of Versigny, not far from Montagny. Louise came of a literary family and early showed a precocious talent for poetry and the arts. After her marriage to the Marquis of Giac she lived near Senlis in the château of Valjenceuse, where her salon was the centre of a small literary circle. She was two years older than Gérard, and it is reasonable to suppose that it was she who first stirred the heart and the imagination of the young poet. Perhaps she was the inspiration for the girl who smiles down on him from a château window in his early poem 'Fantasy' :

> It is an air with which I would not part
> For all Rossini, Weber, and Mozart,
> An ancient air whose melancholy tone
> Possesses secret charms for me alone.
>
> Now every time I hear it played
> My spirit sloughs two centuries;
> I seem to see a green hillside
> Under the sunset's yellowing rays.
>
> A park with a château of brick and stone,
> Its windows with rose reflections lit,
> A river idly flows between
> The meadow flowers at its feet.
>
> At her high window, gazing down,
> A dark-eyed lady with golden hair,
> In antique dress, whom I must have seen
> In a former life . . . I remember her.

It was, however, Gérard's biographer, Aristide Marie, who first revealed that the original of Adrienne was undoubtedly Sophie Dawes, the Baronne de Feuchères. That a mature woman of thirty in the brief course of one casual encounter could have been the first to evoke such intense feelings in a twelve-year-old boy is perhaps surprising, but if we recall Gérard's deep-rooted preoccupation with the image of his lost mother, we can realize his admiration of the great lady who graciously joined in the young folk's dances. All the vague and confusing emotions aroused in him by his young companions who had previously, however unsatisfactorily, partly substituted for his mother, feelings which had led to the first stirrings of a genuine love for Louise, were now suddenly centred upon this new idol. The process of idealization began early, and when we meet her again, Adrienne has become a spirit 'transfigured by her costume as she was already by her vocation'. Who, in reality, was this strange enchantress? Gérard's idol proves, not unnaturally, to have feet of clay.

Sophie Dawes, who came of a poor family of fisherfolk, was born in 1790 at St Helens in the Isle of Wight. Her early history has been traced from a dress-shop where she was first employed, by way of a brothel, to Covent Garden theatre. It was there that she was introduced to the Duc de Bourbon, then on a visit to England. The Duke, thirty-three years her senior, was immediately infatuated. When he returned to France in 1815, he installed her at Chantilly, where she passed for his natural daughter. A husband was found for her in the person of a young officer named Adrien Victor Feuchères, and they were married in 1818. He appears to have been a pleasant and intelligent young man of good appearance and considerable charm. Together with a suitable dowry, he received the title of Baron in 1819. It was not until some time after the marriage that the true relationship between his wife and the Duc de Bourbon was gradually revealed to him. When, however, there could no longer be any doubt, they were separated, officially on the grounds of cruelty. Magnanimously he relinquished the dowry and went to Spain.

The Duke's infatuation continued, and increased to such an extent that, in spite of all her extravagances, he could deny Sophie nothing. She loved to appear in fantastic dresses and to be seen and admired by the people. The hunts she organized, the fêtes and the pageants, were all designed to this end. She was often to be seen riding in the forests and, in the role of the great lady condescending to share the villagers' simple pleasures, she regularly joined in village dances and songs. To the young Gérard, who would thus have seen her on many occasions, she must have appeared a striking and romantic figure, and his imagination endowed this not unusually attractive woman with a far greater beauty than she actually possessed.

Of a dominating and ambitious character, she was determined to establish herself and as the Duke grew older she persuaded him, ostensibly for the purpose of enlarging his hunting-grounds, to acquire part of the domain of Mortefontaine and later that of Saint Sulpice du Désert. Immediately after acquiring these the old Duke made a will in which he left them to Sophie together with the domain of Saint Leu Taverny. Almost exactly a year later, in 1830, the Duke was found dead, hanging from a window fastening in the château of Saint Leu. Two handkerchiefs had been employed, one encircling his neck, the other attaching this to the fastening, and his toes were touching the ground. The discovery of a secret passage connecting the Duke's bedroom with Sophie's lent further support to the suggestion of murder. Sophie was suspected of the crime but her imminent trial was forestalled by the evidence of a doctor who pronounced for suicide. At the same time the old Duke's will was contested by the family and the expensive lawsuits that resulted finally compelled Sophie to sell the property at Saint Sulpice. Later she fell seriously ill and returned to England, where she died in 1840.

Such in real life was the figure that inspired the young Gérard with his ideal of feminine beauty, *biondo e grassoto*, fair-haired and plump after the manner of Rubens, to which he was to remain faithful all his life, and of which his abortive affair with Marie Pleyel was later to seem a betrayal and even a profanation. It was a vision in direct contrast with the 'sweet reality' of the rejected, black-haired 'Sylvie'. Curiously enough, 'Sylvie' was probably more closely related to 'Adrienne' than he could ever have suspected, for when Sophie came to France her younger sister Marie Charlotte Dawes, then eighteen years old, accompanied her. She lived at Mortefontaine and must have been one of Gérard's young companions. But since Sophie was generally accepted as the Duke's daughter, Gérard could never have guessed that Marie Charlotte was her sister.

At the time of the Duke's death, Gérard was occupied with other matters in Paris, but he no doubt learned the circumstances of it, and one may speculate on the coincidence of their close resemblance to those of his own death twenty-five years later. Whether Gérard also knew of the suspicions surrounding the Baroness Adrien is doubtful, but in any case, 'Adrienne' lived on in his memory, to await reincarnation in the later stages of his strange romantic quest.

3

First Literary Friendships

In the general chorus of acclaim that greeted Gérard's first literary productions one voice was lacking. To the staid and stern Dr Labrunie these were frivolous activities, and he looked with alarm and disfavour on his son's growing circle of Bohemian friends. His one aim was to see Gérard set up in a steady and lucrative career. Accordingly, on leaving school, Gérard had been apprenticed to a printer and when this career proved unsuccessful he was entered as a clerk in a neighbouring notary's office. But it was not in his nature to endure the constraint of fixed hours, and it very soon became evident that he was not suited to the work. Finally it was decided that he should follow his father's calling, and he was enrolled in the School of Medicine. For two years he worked hard. He enjoyed his studies, and in later life he recalled with pride the numerous occasions on which he had attended the sick at the Hotel Dieu during the cholera epidemic of 1832 in Paris, when many medical students helped to relieve the shortage of doctors. But although he continued to figure in the list of medical students up to 1834, his attendance had long before then been irregular and at last ceased altogether.

Meanwhile he had continued to contribute both verse and prose to a number of literary journals. He still remained faithful to the classics, and his *Odelettes*, composed at this time, were simple and sincere poems written with delicate artistry in the traditional manner. 'The little odes of Ronsard served me for model,' he says. 'It was moreover a classical form, which he imitated from Anacreon, Bion, and, up to a certain point, Horace. The concentrated form of the Odelette seemed to me no less worthy of preservation than the sonnet.' Gérard also published a selection from the poets of the Pléiade.[1]

But other influences were already at work. The success of his translation of *Faust* encouraged him to try his hand at translating

---

[1] The group of young poets who in the sixteenth century, modelling themselves on Greek and Latin authors, gave new life to French poetry: du Bellay, Ronsard, Baïf, Bellau, Jodelle, de Tyard and Dorat.

other German authors, and in 1830 he published a selection from Klopstock, Goethe, Schiller and Burger, besides a study of the German poets. He was strongly attracted by German romanticism. The influence of Hoffmann is clearly apparent in some of the tales he wrote at this time, such as the *Sonate du Diable* and *Metempsycose,* and it is here that we first find him adopting the theories of Pythagoras on the transmigration of souls, which were to take an ever-increasing hold on his imagination.

Now, however, it was the French romantics who claimed his allegiance. He read Victor Hugo's *Han d'Islande* and was so impressed by the novel that he at once determined to seek the author's permission to dramatize it. Hugo, struck by the younger man's charm and enthusiasm, readily agreed. It was a decisive moment in Gérard's life, for this was the beginning of his endless and frustrating struggle to win fame in the theatre. Through Jules Janin, then the literary editor of the *Quotidienne,* with whom he had formed a firm friendship, he was introduced to Harel, the director of the Odéon theatre, and it was to Harel that Gérard offered the work, Hugo having expressed his satisfaction with it. But the melodrama called for such an elaborate and expensive production that Harel was forced to refuse it.

This set-back in no way interfered with the growing friendship between Gérard and Hugo. Nor did it in the least reduce the former's enthusiasm, to which he sometimes gave extravagant expression. One evening when he and his friends were dining at the Petit Moulin Rouge, a tavern in the Etoile district, he produced a goblet made from a human skull screwed to a drawer handle for a stem. It was, he said, the skull of a drum-major who had been killed at Moscow. The punch was poured and circulated among them noisily. Suddenly Gérard's voice was heard calling loudly to the waiter for sea-water.

'What for?' asked Théophile Gautier in amazement.

'Don't you know', rejoined Célestin Nanteuil, 'that *he* wrote that Han d'Islande drank sea-water from the skulls of the dead. Let us do the same. Waiter! Sea-water!' *He,* of course, was the Master, Victor Hugo, whom they all admired.

The group, the *Petit Cénacle,* usually congregated in du Seigneur's studio, a converted fruit-shop in the Rue de Vaugirard, where they sat about on piles of old cushions drinking punch and debating with enthusiasm. As Gérard explained in a letter to Sainte-Beuve early in 1832, the *Petit Cénacle,* or little coterie, was formed 'solely as a useful association and to provide a select public on whom one could try out one's work in advance. . . . It is also a powerful incentive to be asked every day: what have you been doing? and to have about one people who are working.'

Jean du Seigneur, or Jehan Duseigneur as he styled himself—for it was customary within the group to alter or elaborate bourgeois-sounding names—was then a promising young sculptor. He was twenty years old, small but strongly built. Despite his odd appearance – Théophile Gautier recalls that he wore his dark chestnut hair brushed up from two partings over the temples into points above his forehead 'like the flame which crowns geniuses' – he was a quiet and modest young man. Gautier also relates that what chiefly worried him was his healthy pink and white complexion, because it was the fashion in the romantic school to look pale and hollow-cheeked, as if consumed by passion and remorse. It gave one a fatal, Byronic air, which women found interesting. Although Duseigneur could not achieve this consumptive appearance, his clothes conformed to the young idea. He wore a pointed close-fitting doublet laced behind, a jacket with broad velvet revers and a large knotted silk cravat.

Other members of the group included the sculptor Antoine Auguste Préault, Achille Deveria, artist and engraver, and perhaps more conspicuously, on account of his Malayan complexion, Bouch-ardy, with his great yellow eyes, heavy eyebrows and thin silky beard and moustache, eternally occupied with his involved and incomprehensible poetic dramas. Célestin Nanteuil, already much sought after by editors for his illustrations although still under twenty, was a blue-eyed, fair, slender young man. He wore a long blue coat shaped rather like a soutane, and had all the air of a timid young artist. In contrast, Pierre Borel, Pétrus Borel, the self-styled Werewolf and anarchist, was a grave and imposing figure. He had begun as an architect, but his intractable nature had soon revolted against the restraints of this occupation and he had turned to literature. Lonely and independent, a despiser of society, he found ready acceptance with the group through his enthusiasm for poetry.

Not all of them succeeded in establishing themselves. Jules Vabre, for example, whose fantastic work on 'The Incommodiousness of Commodes' was announced on the cover of Borel's *Rhapsodies*, never achieved publication. Auguste Maquet, on the other hand, later became the collaborator of Alexandre Dumas. At this time, in keeping with the rest, he had changed his name to Auguste MacKeat. The poet Théophile Dondey changed his name by anagram to Philothée O'Neddy, partly because there was already one Théophile in the group. He was a highly-strung, excitable young man, of an aggressive originality which was continually ex-ploding in paradox, hyperbole and extravagant metaphor. He was very short-sighted and was never without his eyeglasses. He would even wear them while he slept, for he said that without them he 'could not distinguish his dreams and lost all the enchantments of the night. The poetic charms of the sylphs, the provocative attractions of the graceful succubi which haunted the happy sleep of his youth retreated into a vague mist.'

Théophile Gautier, long-haired, bearded and exuberant, took his place easily in the group but what of the gentle Gérard, 'the good Gérard' as he was generally called, with his polished manners and reserved language? Gérard, the eternal wanderer, could make himself at home in any company. Those very qualities of gentleness and kindness endeared him to everyone; all were enchanted by his delightful conversation no less than by the sound of his voice which one of his closest friends described as 'so charming that no one who had heard it would ever forget it, so sweetly modulated that one listened to it as to a song'. He was extremely good-looking, with his somewhat pallid complexion, a slender, slightly aquiline nose, firm chin and well-shaped mouth, the lower lip rather full, a sign of kindness and goodwill. His high forehead shone like porcelain, and his delicately shaped head was covered with very fine fair hair like 'golden smoke'. But he stood out among his noisy and ostentatiously eccentric companions by his very inconspicuousness. 'He sought the shade', said his friend Théo, 'with as much care as others seek the light.'

'At that period of eccentricity (again it is Théo speaking) when everyone sought to distinguish himself by some peculiarity of dress – a soft velours hat in the Rembrandt style, a velvet cloak flung over the shoulder, a Van Dyck doublet, a frock coat with fancy braiding round the buttonholes, a braided Hungarian coat, or some other exotic garment – Gérard dressed in the simplest fashion, the most indistinguishable, so to speak, like someone who wished to pass in the crowd without being noticed. In the summer he wore clothes of black Orleans cloth, and in winter a dark blue overcoat chosen to look like anybody else's.'

Even at that time he was inclined to keep his own counsel. He never explained himself to his friends. Perhaps they were even a little in awe of him. 'Sometimes one would catch sight of him at a street corner, hat in hand, in a sort of ecstasy, obviously far withdrawn from his immediate surroundings. . . . When we found him absorbed in this way, we were careful not to accost him bluntly for fear of causing him to fall from the height of his dream like a somnambulist suddenly awakened with a start while walking with eyes closed in deep sleep along the edge of a roof.'

Despite Dr Labrunie's understandable alarm at the unconventional dress and behaviour of his son's companions, they were for the most part fundamentally serious-minded young men filled with a keen desire to give new life to the arts. Gérard, who shared their ardour and could himself on occasion, as we have seen, give extravagant expression to it, describes their situation as one in which 'there was a medley of activity, indecision and idleness, of splendid utopias, philosophic or religious aspirations and vague enthusiasms, mingled with some impulses towards rebirth; of boredom with past discords and of uncertain hopes.' It was a time of instability and uncertainty when many of the younger generation had retreated into their ivory towers, but they emerged in force to support the cause of Romanticism at the famous battle of Hernani.

The contest was between classic and romantic, between reason and feeling, between on the one hand reliance on custom, tradition, purity of language and the three unities, and on the other the impulse to break away from convention, to open up new horizons, to broaden the scope of expression by introducing foreign and exotic influences and to find a new creative freedom.

For the moment Gérard was caught up in the tide of Romanticism. The announcement of the forthcoming production of Hugo's *Hernani* had already caused a stir. It was widely discussed in the cafés, and Hugo foresaw that it would meet with a good deal of opposition, because it flouted all the accepted conventions of the drama. He would need all the support he could get for the première of his play. Gérard, being in the Master's confidence, was entrusted with the task of rallying the band of young supporters. With the help of Pétrus Borel, he eagerly prepared for the occasion.

Naturally Théophile Gautier was one of the first to join Gérard's little army of recruits; and, since to express a general revolt against convention was the purpose of the occasion, he was at pains to appear in as startling an outfit as he could contrive. The principal feature of it was, of course, the famous red waistcoat, and he related with some humour how his tailor received the order. 'He thought I was mad, but out of respect for the family he refrained from giving expression to his thoughts, contenting himself with a timid objection.' Overruled by Théo's nonchalant assurance, the tailor asked him to choose the cloth, whereupon Théo pulled out a roll of magnificent red silk and unrolled it, turning it this way and that to catch the light. In spite of the tailor's horror and scandalization, the order was duly executed. The rest of the outfit, Gautier tells us, consisted of 'pale green trousers with black velvet seams, a black jacket with lightly turned velvet revers, and a plain grey overcoat lined with green satin. A silk band, serving for a cravat and shirt collar, was fastened round the neck.' 'The costume,' he

B

concludes, 'it must be agreed, was not badly designed to irritate and scandalize the philistines.'

The philistines were duly shocked but such an ostentatious exhibition of eccentricity can have served no purpose beyond that of outraging an audience already prepared for innovations. On the night of 25 February 1830, Gérard distributed among the confederates tickets marked with the password *hierro*. Armed with these they entered the theatre long before the play was due to begin and distributed themselves in groups about the auditorium. 'It would have been enough', wrote Gautier, 'to admit us one hour before the public; but, with perfidious intent, doubtless in the hope of some disturbance which might necessitate or provide a pretext for the intervention of the police, the doors were opened at two in the afternoon, so that there were eight hours to wait before the raising of the curtain.' When *Hernani* was finally performed, the enthusiastic applause of the younger generation led by Gérard's followers had its effect and despite the enmity of the opposition, despite the clamorous criticisms, the interruptions and the general uproar, the play was an acclaimed success. The battle was won and Romanticism thus firmly established.

Already the pattern of Gérard's double life was beginning to emerge. Though generally to be distinguished among his companions by his quiet behaviour, he readily joined in their riotous evenings in the taverns and was on one occasion arrested with some of them for disturbing the peace, and spent the night in gaol. The part of the young Bohemian he had chosen to play was out of character, but he was determined to emulate his friends. Janin wrote that 'he was intoxicated with the genius of his friends, as one is intoxicated with the beauty of one's mistress.' Doubtless he found that only under the influence of liquor could he give expression to his natural exuberance, which was normally severely repressed by his timidity. Throughout his life and in every aspect of it a strange dichotomy can be observed. Always there was an internal conflict of opposites, between religion and scepticism, past and present, imagination and reality, dream and life. This conflict was to be the principal cause of his restlessness, and his whole life can be seen as an attempt to resolve it.

A parallel struggle can be traced in Gérard's professional career. By instinct a traditionalist, he was excited by the new prospects offered by the Romantics and allied himself with their cause. But in his own writing with its simplicity of expression and purity of language he remained true to the classical ideal. In his enthusiasm for *Han d'Islande* he had early turned his hand to drama. He was tenacious and determined and, just as the friendships he formed remained to the end, so did his ambition to succeed as a dramatist.

Undeterred by the refusal of his dramatized version of Hugo's novel, he set to work on a verse drama, *Villon l'Ecolier*. When this met with the same fate he began *Nicolas Flamel,* a prose drama inspired by *Faust*. Disappointed again, he produced *Le Prince des Sots,* two acts in verse, the principal part of which, according to Gautier, consisted of a sort of Gothic mystery. We have only his account of it, for the manuscript is lost. Gérard offered it first to the Théatre Français without success. However, his hopes were renewed when it was favourably received at the Odéon. The committee stipulated only that a prologue should be supplied explaining the mystery. Gérard applied to Théo, who was quick at such tasks. The prologue was written and the play at last accepted. Still it was not produced. As time went on Gérard began to grow impatient. Harel, the director of the theatre, prevaricated. Gérard must think of his future, he said. So short a piece, produced in conjunction with others, might tend to be overlooked. It was far better to make one's debut with a full five-act play. Gérard, always docile, was easily persuaded. This time he confided the plot of a new drama to Gautier and they agreed to collaborate. But *La Dame de Carouge* met with as little success as Gérard's previous efforts. His next attempt was a comedy in three acts, *Tartuffe chez Molière* which was again accepted by the Odéon but never produced. Gérard persisted with *Lara,* a tragedy in one act, possibly inspired by Byron's poem. In offering it to the Théatre Français he pinned his hopes on the economy of the production it demanded. 'It can be produced without the least expense, with four actors,' he wrote in a letter to the director. He was again refused, but very soon he was at work on a three-act comedy, *Jodelet,* and was revolving other dramatic projects in his head.

He was still contributing to various journals, sometimes anonymously, sometimes under different pseudonyms. Although he also often signed himself 'G' or 'Gérard', he never used his full name for his literary productions. The pseudonym that he finally fixed upon and by which he was to become known did not appear until 1835, but an earlier pseudonym, Louis Gerval, shows that he had already considered deriving a name from the plot of land at Mortefontaine where he had spent his earliest years. It was, perhaps, a form of protest at having been snatched away from that Eden from which he now felt himself for ever excluded. At the same time it was respect for Dr Labrunie and fear of offending him that compelled Gérard to refrain from associating the name of Labrunie with that side of his life of which he knew his father disapproved.

He was well aware that Dr Labrunie regarded his literary

proclivities with suspicion, not merely because it distracted him from a 'serious occupation' but because it might lead him into bad company, a suspicion doubly confirmed when Gérard was again arrested with some of his friends as they made their way home through the streets of Paris, still lustily singing, after a lively evening at the tavern where 'the shouting, the fists beating on the table, the songs yelled at the top of their voices made the pots and plates rattle on the shelves.' It was 1 February 1832, the night of the discovery of the Legitimist plot in the Rue des Prouvaires. This conspiracy, led by a shoemaker who lived in the Rue des Prouvaires, aimed at invading the Tuileries and capturing the royal family.

At that time there was general unrest among the young. The more politically-minded, supporters of the republicans who looked for the overthrow of the monarchy, formed themselves into groups and roamed the streets, armed with clubs. Their enemies were the shopkeepers and the middle classes in general. They wore their hair close-cropped and were to be distinguished by the small round leather hats they affected, from which they were known as *bousingots*. The *Jeune France,* on the other hand, to which group Gérard and his friends belonged, while they too detested the standards and conventions of the middle classes and although some of them, like Théo, were at least in theory ardent republicans, were almost solely interested in literature and the arts. Though, in contrast to the *bousingots,* they wore beards and long hair, sometimes down to their shoulders, they often looked wild enough and were frequently confused with them.

On such a night of alarums and excursions it is no wonder that Gérard's noisy band was arrested along with many other suspects. They were taken to the lock-up at the Palais-Royal. There they were separated. After eighteen hours without food or attention of any sort Gérard was removed to the prison of Saint Pélagie, and it was only several days later that, after a summary enquiry, he was declared innocent of any involvement in the plot, and released.

4

Gay Bohemia

In early 1834 Gérard was still living with his father in the Rue St Martin. He had until now made a show of serious study, but more and more of his time was being taken up with his friends and his writing. Gérard did his best to alleviate the growing tension between father and son by a display of filial devotion, inspired by a genuine affection but also partly by a sense of guilt. Gautier records how at the battle of *Hernani* Gérard 'installed his men, applauded conscientiously and went off to pay his duty to his father who went to bed at nine.' When Théo expressed his astonishment at such behaviour 'on such an evening as this', Gérard replied, 'Even if I had written *Hernani.*' Throughout his life he showed the same regard for his father, both in his regular visits to the house when he was in Paris and in his constant correspondence during his travels.

Dr Labrunie was in his own way a devoted father. Gérard was the one substantial link with his wife left to him. But during those years of hardship abroad the child had grown away from him. Some traits of the mother were discernible in her son, but these formed only a tenuous thread to bind together two essentially opposed natures. So far the course of their relationship had been comparatively smooth, but now an event occured which helped to estrange them further. Gérard's grandmother, whom he had loved deeply and sincerely as the closest connection with his mother, had died in 1828. Now in January six years later his grandfather also died and Gérard inherited half the property. His share of the proceeds amounted to thirty thousand francs, a not inconsiderable sum. At twenty-five, he suddenly found himself financially independent and so free to choose his own way of life.

We do not know what Dr Labrunie said on this occasion but, in view of Gérard's sympathetic account of how this same grandfather once left home to settle at Mortefontaine, we may surmise it was enough to confirm Gérard in his own resolution. In April he left his father's house and went to live with his friend Célestin Nanteuil in the Rue de Vaugirard. This decision was to cause

Gérard endless remorse. Again and again in his letters to his father he attempts to vindicate his choice of a career. In one he points to his success in earning his livelihood by his pen and making a name for himself; in another he excuses himself: 'I understand all that the deceptions suffered, the fears and perhaps the bruised tenderness of a father's or a mother's heart can mean; but alas! does not the eternal history of this kind of situation show that in such cases there is a destiny that cannot be overruled?' Towards the end of his life he expressed his regret that his father had never really understood him.

Dr Labrunie remained unmoved. Even in the most difficult times, he gave his son no financial assistance. His wife's dowry, held in trust for Gérard, was never paid to him, and even the small allowance made him for a year or two from this source was withdrawn. Possibly he did not even trouble to answer his son's frequent letters from abroad, for in one Gérard asks 'Have you received all my letters? I have had none from you, but perhaps they have got lost.' Nevertheless there was a very real feeling of mutual affection, at least in the early years. Houssaye relates how 'Gérard crossed the paternal threshold with great respect, embraced the old surgeon and said to him, in a voice which went straight to the heart of any who heard it, "Good evening, father". Sunday and Thursday were two fête days for both of them. Dinner was leisurely and they talked a great deal. After dinner, Gérard shook the dust a little from some of the books; sometimes he conducted his father to the café Turc; but he did not stay there; for as soon as he had breathed the air of the street again, he was off without saying goodnight. When he was in Paris, he never missed dinner with his father on Sunday and Thursday; but how many times his father waited for him in vain. . . . None the less the cover was laid for this prodigal son in the earlier years. That would bring him back, his father said. And he dined sadly with the memory of the charming vagabond.'

Although Gérard did not come into full possession of his inheritance until the end of December 1834, he was able meanwhile to realize the dream he had long cherished of a visit to Italy. With the meagre funds at his disposal, the journey demanded strict economy, and he determined to travel by boat and stage-coach and on foot. Depositing what funds he had with Duseigneur, the only one of his friends who had a desk with a lock, to be forwarded to him as required, he set off in September for the south of France. Having seen Avignon and Vaucluse, he followed the banks of the Durance to Aix, and so by way of Antibes he arrived at Nice. 'I enclose', he wrote to Duseigneur from Nice in October, 'a letter which I beg you to post on to my father, but so that nothing may indicate where it comes from, nor how. I have dated it from Provence, because I shall not tell him I have been to Italy until I return. That would disturb him. I am supposed to be travelling to see Provence.' At length he crossed the border into Italy, and, after visiting Genoa and Florence where he 'admired the cathedral and baptistry, and the masterpieces of Michelangelo', he went on to Pisa and thence by Spoleto to Rome. Finally he embarked at Civita Vecchia for Naples, the final objective of his journey.

He stayed ten days in Naples, but the account of his experiences there given in *Octavie,* which was written eight years later, is factually unreliable. Nevertheless there is some reason to believe that he may have met there the young English girl, the 'syren of the grottoes', whom he presents 'biting with her ivory teeth into the skin of a lemon'. Certain characteristics impressed him so strongly that they became part of his private mythology. That Octavie, like Adrienne, is a composite figure, there can be no doubt, but some such real encounter at Naples may have played a part in the story. Gérard probably visited Herculaneum and Pompeii on this occasion. His readings in his beloved Apuleius would inevitably have drawn him to the temple of Isis in the latter.

Unfortunately the money he was expecting to receive at Naples did not arrive and with empty pockets he had no choice but to return to Marseilles, where he settled himself in a hotel to live on credit until the money should come through. But on 4 November he was still waiting and he wrote to his friend, 'If all else fails . . . if Paris has been buried in an earthquake or the Bank has been blown up, or Mignotte has committed suicide; you yourself Jehan Duseigneur crushed like Don Juan by your own statues, if there is no more money in the world, if there are no more notaries, no more stock-brokers, no more bankers (which I should like but can scarcely hope for), let me know in a letter addressed to Marseilles.' A week later he wrote to his friends, 'I hardly dare walk because my boots are splitting. . . . But I have dined well all the time: imagine, I have eaten nothing but macaroni and fruit for a fortnight.' Eventually the money arrived, and he was able to move on to Agen, where he was warmly welcomed by his cousin Gautié, a wine merchant who had previously on a visit to Paris been introduced by Gérard to his circle. To the end of his life Gautié retained a proud and happy memory of his acquaintance with the *Jeune France,* and he was delighted to see Gérard again.

But already Gérard was eager to be back in Paris, to embark on the new life he had planned for himself, that of the fashionable young literary man-about-town. Rich as he now considered himself, he had every prospect of enjoying life to the full, and he was determined to make the most of it. There was to be no more study. The retiring student was transformed into a dandy with light-coloured gloves, well-tailored coat, and green or yellow trousers strapped beneath patent leather shoes. Yet there was always some small negligence here or there about this elegant, artistocratic-looking figure which betrayed the dreamer, and his habit of stuffing his pockets was not always conducive to a neat appearance. Gautier tells us that 'he usually wore a sort of frock-coat of a brilliant black material with huge pockets in which he hid a library of old books picked up here and there, five or six notebooks and a whole quantity of scraps of paper on which he wrote down in a fine small hand the ideas which he caught on the wing during his long walks.' Much later Gérard himself wrote in a letter, 'The reason why I cannot work in Paris is that I write only by rapture and caprice, and for this liberty and the open air are necessary.' His roamings about the Valois countryside in his young days and those early-morning excursions with his father's batman had given him a taste for walking which never left him. It was in part an expression of his restless nature. 'His body [again it is Théo speaking] seemed to skim the earth, swept along by the wings of his spirit. One would have said that he hovered above reality, sustained by his dream.' Yet he was an acute observer of everything about him, requiring the continual spur of the sights and sounds of real life to stimulate his imagination.

On his return to Paris he had settled in with one of his most recent friends, Camille Rogier, a successful young illustrator, in the Rue des Beaux Arts but when shortly afterwards they were joined by Arsène Houssaye, they began to look about for more spacious quarters. It was Rogier who found the very place to suit them. At that time, in a hollow between the Louvre and the Place du Carrousel, a narrow cul-de-sac descended at right angles to the Seine. This was the Rue du Doyenné. Here in one of the old sixteenth-century houses, already for the most part uninhabited, the landlord agreed to rent them a vast room with four double doors, which had formerly been occupied by the dean of the canons who had officiated at the now-ruined chapel of the Doyenné, the old church of St Thomas du Louvre. On one side the windows overlooked the cul-de-sac which ended in a little square sheltered by trees beneath the still-imposing ruins. On the other side they commanded a view of the sculptured façade of the museum, seen through the foliage of the trees in a large, uncultivated garden. Here five or six horses grazed peacefully, together with two cows, four donkeys and a multitude of chickens, geese, ducks and pigeons. The whole quarter was in process of gradual demolition. Balzac, who knew it well, describes it in his *Cousine Bette* : 'the shadows, the silence, the icy air, the cavernous depth of the ground level, combine to make of these houses a sort of crypts or living tombs. . . . One finds oneself asking who can live there, what happens there in the evening, at an hour when this alley is changed into a haunt of cut-throats, where all the vices of Paris are given free rein under the cloak of night.' Dilapidated the place certainly was, but scarcely sinister, and it was to know a last brief period of riotous gaiety before its final demolition. No sooner had the three friends taken possession of their new quarters than the process of transformation began. The shutters of the old room were thrown open, light flooded in through the high windows and the work of redecoration immediately began.

Théo, who lived nearby, spent all his days there. Other friends flocked in, Célestin Nanteuil, Pétrus Borel, Philothée O'Neddy among the first; Edouard Ourliac, the comedian, Emile Vattier, Henry Egmont whose translation of Hoffmann's *Tales* Rogier was then engaged in illustrating; Auguste de Chatillon, Roger de Beauvoir, Alphonse Esquiros, and many others.

Suddenly the great room had awoken. The very walls had come alive with fantastic coloured figures. Here, Chasseriau's *Bacchante* held tigers in leash like dogs; there, de Chatillon's *Red Monk* read his bible propped against the curved hip of a naked, sleeping woman. Vattier's *Watteau* was accompanied by two long panels representing landscapes of Provence by Corot. Rogier, perched on a ladder, smiled into his beard as he busily painted a Neptune with his own features above a mirror. It was not without some temerity that Gérard introduced amongst the works of his young artist friends two panels by Fragonard which he had picked up for fifty francs, and it speaks well for his more liberal influence that these then outmoded paintings were not rejected out of hand. Amid all this activity the young poets enthusiastically recited their verses. The doors burst open and Théo entered. A Louis XIII chair was brought forward but promptly collapsed under his weight and another had to be produced before he could take his turn. The room was alive with youthful energy and eagerness. There was much serious discussion, but there was also gaiety and laughter. There was dancing and singing, too, and above all were heard the musical voices and laughter of the *Cydalises*, a name conferred on them by Gérard after the *comédiennes* and dancers of the Regency period.

First among these was Rogier's mistress. He painted her portrait on the wall in a dress of filemont, a sad presage of her early death.

Théo also fell madly in love with her and in the heat of his romantic passion even spoke of killing his rival. She was a continual cause of contention between the two friends but when she died they were reconciled in a common despair. There were also Lorry, the young actress from the Opéra, Victorine, and Sylvanie Plessy who had been engaged by the Comédie-Française at sixteen. And there was also Esquiros's wife, already becoming known as a writer under her maiden name of Adèle Battanchon. 'We were young,' writes Gérard in his *Petits Châteaux de Bohème,* 'always gay, sometimes rich,' and again, 'What happy times! There were balls, suppers, fancy-dress parties – we played old comedies, in which Miss Plessy, then at the threshold of her career, did not disdain to take a part' – it was that of Beatrice in *Jodelet* (a comedy in the seventeenth-century manner, written by Gérard himself, which never achieved production outside the Rue du Doyenné).

Gautier, Rogier and Houssaye observed fixed hours for work, beginning punctually at seven in the morning. That was not Gérard's way. So far he had produced nothing of any note since his translation, save perhaps for *La Main de Gloire*, reprinted later as *La Main Enchantée*, a tale in which fantasy and humour are deftly mingled but of no very great literary value. He showed no promise of ever becoming anything more than a hack writer of ephemeral articles.

His friends delighted in his company, but he moved among them as a somewhat enigmatic figure. He joined quietly in all their festivities, but he also lived a life apart into which they never penetrated. He would spend whole nights wandering about Paris from one tavern to another, from Pantin to Paul Niquet's ('dingy Paris, some would call it disreputable Paris', as he says in the *Nuits d'Octobre*), from the quarries of Montmartre where he chatted with the lime-burners, to the market, a hive of activity long before dawn with the country carts arriving and unloading in endless succession. Was he in love, his friends asked themselves, and with whom? With women he was gallant and courteous, but still shy, 'Blushing like Psyche and at the least approach of love folding himself in his wings', as Théo put it. He would suddenly become fascinated by women he saw in the distance, but would never approach them for fear of destroying his illusion.

That there were passing attractions is beyond question. Gérard himself relates the story of one such:

About 1835 Alexandre Dumas had a mistress for whose beautiful eyes I was dying of love. I have always respected the wives of my friends: but this one was not a wife. The irresistible charm she had for me did not dispel the consciousness of my treachery. I hesitated to declare myself . . . one day, going up to Dumas', I met him on the stairs. He said to me 'Come with me to the shooting gallery, we'll come back to lunch afterwards.'

I am rather short-sighted, but I have a good eye: we hit bulls-eyes, we broke dolls. Dumas complimented me, yet all the same I hardly knew how to hold the pistol. Suddenly he asked the attendant for something. The latter pressed a button. A little jet of water sprang from the middle of a stone cup and rose two or three feet above the ground. The attendant went to get a coloured glass ball and delicately placed it on the tip of the jet of water.

What a surprise! The glass ball turned, rose and fell, and hovered in the air like a swallow in the rain. Dumas with one glance and one shot shattered the ball and asked for another, I missed, he broke it, and this happened six times in succession. When he had broken his half-dozen balls, he said to me: 'It's a good morning exercise; let's go and have lunch.'

On the way back I was furious; the moral was clear to me and I said to myself: how in fact can I get rid of this colossus? To strike him from behind would not be fair. . . . He may not be so expert with the sword but he has such great legs and such huge arms! Let's be prudent and avoid all possibility of a duel – with Alexander Dumas . . .'

It is hard to believe that the gentle Gérard ever really harboured such designs against his friend, but the infatuation was authentic enough.

However Adrienne was not forgotten. He was still faithful to the memory of that pure and ideal love, but she was translated into the world of dream. While he cherished a vague passion for the unattainable, he was more and more coming to separate his idea of love from any real object, in his own words 'to forsake the prize for the shadow'. And then one evening at the Variétés theatre he saw a beautiful young actress. Enhanced by the artificial glamour of the scene, the young woman's smile, and her voice, soft yet firm and vibrant, filled him with happiness. In his eyes she was 'beautiful as the day in the blaze of the footlights lighting her from below, pale as the night when the lowered footlights left her lighted from above in the rays of the spotlight, when she appeared more natural, shining in the shadow of her own beauty. . . . She realized in the flesh my divine and ideal dream.' His star had risen again. It was Adrienne reincarnated. Haloed by the spotlight, she stood there tangibly before him, but at the same time remote and un-untouchable as in a dream. Some years later, recalling the romantic attitude he had adopted at this time, he was to write, 'we were drunk with poetry and love. Love, alas, of vague forms, rose and blue tints, metaphysical phantoms! In our simplicity the real woman, seen at close quarters, filled us with aversion; she must appear as queen or goddess, and above all must not approach too near.'

Every evening he returned to the theatre to renew his delight and to pay tribute to his idol. This, then, was the love that distracted him. One day in Turaine he bought a great four-poster bed with Renaissance pillars and embroidered hangings. It was said to have been the bed used by Marguerite de Valois at Tours in the sixteenth century. When it arrived in the Rue du Doyenné, the entrance had to be enlarged to get it in. Gérard slept on a mattress on the floor at its foot, for as Janin relates, 'having bought and paid for the bed, he hadn't enough money to furnish it.' Someone once asked him 'Who sleeps there?', to which Gerard promptly replied 'My imagination'. It is this same bed of which Balzac speaks in *Honorine* : 'I have been told of a poet who, madly in love with a singer, at the onset of his passion bought the most beautiful bed in Paris, without knowing how the actress would react to his love.' His friends joked about it, and it was even said that he had spent eight thousand francs on it. That, as Gérard said, was 'a little exaggerated'.

Nevertheless he was squandering his inheritance, and it was Balzac who suggested that it might be put to better use in founding a periodical. The idea appealed to Gérard; it promised to provide him with a regular source of income, and it would give him an opportunity to swell the reputation of his idol with the public and perhaps even to win her favour. His paper, devoted exclusively to the theatre, was to be a production in every way worthy of her. He set about the task with energy and enthusiasm. Though nominally under the editorship of Frédéric Soulié, the *Monde Dramatique* was inspired solely by Gérard. It was he who arranged everything and collected the contributors, including of course all his friends of the Rue du Doyenné : Dumas, Gautier, Roger de Beauvoir, Egmont, Burat de Gurgy and, as illustrators, Nanteuil, Rogier, Vattier, Lorentz, Leleux. He obtained several articles from Berlioz, and drew in Alphonse Karr whom he now met for the first time. 'One day', says Karr, 'a young man presented me with a card with the name Gérard Labrunie. His pleasant intelligent face, his distinguished manners sufficiently prepossessed me in his favour. He told me he was going to found the *Monde Dramatique,* a really literary and artistic review, on fine Dutch paper, with rare and costly engravings which he had been collecting for some time.

He proposed that I should report two or three theatres of my own choice.'

The first number appeared in May 1835. It was indeed a sumptuous production, and in subsequent numbers praise of the actress duly increased until, aided by this publicity, in April of the following year she appeared with triumphant success at the Opéra Comique. Gérard's ambition for her was achieved, but the review was not a financial success and in June he had to abandon it, having not only lost all his money but having accumulated a debt which was to weigh heavily on him for the rest of his life.

It was the end, too, of the gay life in the Rue du Doyenné. The climax of that had been the *Bal des Truands,* the Tramps' Ball of 28 November 1835. All the more distinguished tenants in the block were invited. There were ambassadors' attachés in blue coats with gold buttons, civil servants and budding young ministers of state with their female companions. An invitation was also sent to the superintendant of police, this being deemed politic to ensure his good will, but he politely refused. It was a splendid moonlit night, and everyone was in the highest of spirits. Only the landlords and concierges were left to snatch what little sleep they could, though there was small chance of rest, for the night was disturbed by the noisy strains of a tavern orchestra engaged for the occasion and by the wild boundings of a monster *galop* from hall to stairs, from stairs to street, and so to the tavern in the tree-sheltered square at the end of the cul-de-sac.

Gérard alone was preoccupied. He had conceived the idea of an opera, *La Reine de Saba,* in which the part of 'the immortal Balkis' should be taken by the actress he adored. Meyerbeer had had great success at the Opéra, and, if he could be interested in it, the piece would be made. Dumas had arranged an appointment for Gérard with Meyerbeer at seven on the following morning. All through the night, in the midst of all the festivities, he could think of nothing but the approaching interview. In his *Petits Châteaux de Bohème,* addressing his friend Arsène Houssaye, Gérard writes of the occasion :

A woman, whom you remember no doubt, was shedding bitter tears in a corner of the room and could not, any more than I, make up her mind to dance. This weeping beauty was unable to hide her grief. Suddenly she caught me by the arm and said : 'Take me away, I can't stay here.'

Giving her my arm I escorted her out. There was not a carriage in the square. I advised her to calm herself and dry her eyes and then go back to the ball; she would only agree to walk in the little square.

I knew how to open a certain board door which gave onto the grazing-ground, and we talked for a long time in the moonlight, under the limes. She told me all her troubles in some detail.

The man who had brought her had fallen in love with another; an intimate quarrel had thereupon arisen between them, and she had threatened to go back either alone or accompanied by someone else; he had replied that she could do as she liked. Hence the sighs and tears.

It was almost dawn. The great saraband was beginning. Three or four historical painters, by nature little given to dancing, had had the little tavern opened and were singing loudly. . . . Our retreat was soon invaded by several masks who had found the little door open. There was talk of going to breakfast at Madrid – the Madrid in the Bois de Boulogne – as we did sometimes. Soon the signal was given, we were swept away, and we set off on foot, escorted by three French guards, of whom two were simply M. d'Egmont and M. De Beauvoir; the third was Giraud, painter in ordinary to the French guards.

The sentries of the Tuileries could not understand this un-expected apparition, which seemed the phantasm of a scene of a hundred years ago, when the French guards would have been leading a party of noisy masqueraders to the lock-up. More-over one of the two little tobacco-sellers, who were so pretty and who were the ornament of our balls, dared not allow herself to be led off to Madrid without informing her husband, who was looking after the house.

We accompanied her through the streets. She knocked on the door. The husband appeared at a window on the mezzanine. She called to him : 'I am going to breakfast with these gentle-men.'

He replied : 'Go to the devil! Fancy waking me up for that!'

The disconsolate beauty put up a feeble enough resistance to being led off to Madrid and, as for me, I took my leave of Rogier explaining to him that I wanted to go and work on my scenario. 'What! You're not coming with us? This lady has no other escort but you . . . and she has chosen you to take her home.'—'But I have an appointment at seven with Meyerbeer, you understand.'

Rogier burst out laughing. He had given one arm to the *Cydalise*; he offered the other to the fair lady, who bowed to me with a slightly mocking air. At least I had served to induce a smile after her tears.

I had given up the prize for the shadow . . . as always!

Unluckily for Gérard, Meyerbeer was occupied with Dumas's *Les Frères corses,* and Gérard's own project had no more than a distant prospect of acceptance. When he had written one act, he learned that the two men had quarrelled and that their agreement had been broken. Dumas left for a voyage in the Mediterranean and Meyerbeer went off to Germany. Gérard's libretto was forgotten. The opera was never written. Abandoned by all, it became a simple oriental tale which forms part of the 'Nuits de Rhamazan' in the *Voyage en Orient.*

The brief bright season of the Rue du Doyenné was over. The landlord, unable to reconcile himself to the Bohemian way of life of his young tenants, gave them notice. The pictures, the tapestries, the Renaissance bed, the clock with a golden dome supported by caryatids and a figure of Diana leaning on a stag in bas-relief, the Medici console table, the carved sideboards, all were dispersed. 'Where did you lose so many beautiful things?' Balzac asked Gérard some time afterwards. 'In misfortunes,' was the reply.

In fact he was able to save some items, but most of the proceeds went towards paying off his debts. Meanwhile the walls were distempered over to hide the shocking nudities that the young artists had left there. Before very long the whole picturesque quarter of the Place du Carrousel was to be demolished. Visiting the spot some years later, Gérard remarked nostalgically 'Our palace has been razed to the ground', and for him, as he picked his way among the debris, it was as if the basis of his real life had crumbled with it.

5

The Star

Gérard's ideal of feminine beauty was that of the paintings of the Italian school. 'For me a Medici,' he notes in the *Carnet de Voyage*, and in *Quintus Aucler* he describes Catherine de Medici admiringly as 'noble and alluring . . . beautiful as Venus and faithful as Artemis . . . so young, so loving, and so pure'.

The young actress who embodied for him the 'eternal type' of beauty was Jenny Colon. Her real name was Marguerite. She was born at Boulogne on 5 November 1808, and was thus little less than six months younger than Gérard. Her parents were actors in a provincial touring company. By about 1820 however they were in Paris, for Jenny's mother and elder sister were both then playing at the Opéra Comique, and it was there two years later that Jenny herself made her first appearance in the part of a child, for which she was singled out largely on account of her golden ringlets. In 1823 she made her debut at the Vaudeville theatre. Jenny was still only sixteen when, during a tour in England, she fell in love with an actor named Lafont, and they were married at Gretna Green. But the marriage did not last long. They had scarcely returned to France after the tour before both parties agreed to have it annulled. Indeed few people knew of it, and Jenny remained Miss Jenny Colon.

During the ten years following Jenny played both in Paris theatres and on tour. She was much admired by the young gallants of the day and there were rumours of many affairs. It was even said that her absences from the theatre from time to time were due to the exigencies of maternity. In 1834 and 1835 she was playing regularly at the Variétés theatre in Paris. By then she was already renowned for her beauty and talent. Her grace, her delicate complexion, her golden hair and dark eyes, as also her voice, enchanted the majority of the public. In a volume, edited by Esquiros, devoted to the beautiful women of Paris, Gautier introduced a portrait of her to please Gérard :

Jenny, who, at first sight, recalls the allegorical figures of the life of Catherine de Medici, possesses something rarer and more elegant than the ordinary type of Flemish beauty, imagined rather than copied by Rubens. She is full-figured and robust, but far from resembling the plump avalanches of human flesh of the painter of Antwerp, her pure and delicate complexion has something of the silky softness of a camellia petal or of rice-paper, and is not lined with a bluish network marked with patches of red like those of the stout divinities of the artist of the Netherlands. She is nearer to the type of the *biondo e grassoto* celebrated by Gozzi. Her sort of beauty appears in some of Paul Veronese's Magdalens, in some of Giorgione's portraits, and in Allori's Judith. Her broad, full, rounded forehead, much more developed than is usual in women, takes the light well and holds it, glistening and playing softly there; the small slender nose, slightly aquiline and almost regal, pleasantly tempers the rather extravagant gaiety of the rest of her face. And, charming singularity, dark pupils sparkle beneath extremely soft light brows of a velvety texture. As for the mouth, it is clean-cut and well-shaped with a slightly mocking curve of the lower lip, which gives it great charm. The oval of her cheeks is distinguished by the graceful fullness of their contours and the absence of prominent cheekbones : the chin is stamped with a dimple in the middle, an excellent love nest, as a poet of the time of Louis XV would have said.

The verdict was not unanimous. There were some who said that the slender nose praised by Théo looked like a comma, and Maxime du Camp in his *Souvenirs Littéraires* described her as a 'plump white actress, with dubiously blonde hair, of little apparent distinction . . . a Dulcinea whose Toboso was by no means an inaccessible realm.' But Théo's overall assessment of her was generally accepted. On the stage, in early seventeenth-century costume, she was the very personification of the dark-eyed, fair-haired lady in antique dress whom Gérard had visualized in the poem 'Fantasy' and so, by extension, she was Adrienne, more particularly the Baroness Adrien de Feuchères, whom in many respects she resembled.

It was in the spring of 1835 that Gérard discovered her, just when he was beginning to draw on his inheritance. He was therefore able to indulge his infatuation. Even before his journey to Italy he had a regular stall at the theatre and every evening saw him ensconced there waiting for the moment when her appearance on the stage would suddenly bring everything to life for him. It was for her sake that he now took so much care about his appearance, although as yet she was not even aware of her ardent but mute admirer. For a year he was content to worship at a distance. 'I was afraid to disturb the magic mirror in which I saw her image,' he confesses in *Sylvie*. Renewed every evening, his absorption with this illusion of perfection grew stronger. His long preoccupation with the confused figure of Adrienne, combined with his early leaning towards Pythagorism, suggested to him that he had found reincarnated his eternal love, not only once briefly encountered years before, but perhaps known and remembered from a former existence. There was even something titillating in the idea of loving a nun in the form of an actress : 'what if they were actually the same ! – There is enough in the suggestion to drive one mad ! It has the fatal attraction by which the unknown lures you like a will-o'-the-wisp over the reeds of a still water.' But Gérard was now in debt and, although he would sometimes send Jenny bouquets anonymously, he had nothing to offer her beyond his devotion.

In an attempt to pay the debts he had contracted, he had turned to journalism. He was still contributing to a number of periodicals and his friends rallied to help him. Théophile Gautier shared with him his column in *La Presse,* and Alphonse Karr, then principal editor of *Figaro,* made him a regular contributor. But from now on Gérard's livelihood was to be precarious. He was now dependent entirely on his pen and the continual strain of having to produce copy prevented him from completing any major literary work until towards the end of his life.

Much later in a letter to his father he looked back on this time regretfully :

Literary work comprises two things : the drudgery of journalism which provides a very good living and an assured position to all who pursue it assiduously, but which unhappily leads no higher and no further. Then the work of books, the theatre, poetical studies, things slow and difficult, which always require very long preliminary labours and some periods of meditation and work without result; but there, also, lies a future, advancement, a happy and honoured old age.

Men of letters who, like Lamartine, Chateaubriand, De Vigny, Casimir Lavigne, Hugo, had incomes, wealth, in short a livelihood assured from elsewhere, are the ones who have made most money, because they had it to begin with and were not forced to divert all their energies to sterile work such as romances and journalism, which is tempting because of its facility.

It is a great misfortune for me that, seven years ago, when I had a sufficient sum of money, although not enough to live on as income, I had not the maturity of mind that today enables me to produce some works of a little note ! But then I had no confidence in myself : I tried a speculation in publishing, in the hope that its success would at least provide me with the means of producing literature later, without fear of starving.

It was unfortunate, too, that he continued to pin his hopes on the theatre. In spite of his previous disappointments, it still seemed to him to promise good remuneration, but now his major concern was to serve the lady of his choice. Already he had envisaged Jenny as Balkis, the Queen of the South, but his immediate task was to plan a more practicable role for her which should help her towards pre-eminence in her profession. Accordingly he entered into an agreement with Dumas as collaborator in a series of productions, each to be signed alternately by one of the partners. They set to work immediately on *Piquillo*, which was to be credited to Dumas as author. Meanwhile Gérard had undertaken to write, in conjunction with Théo, the *Confessions galantes de deux gentilhommes périgourdins*, which, however, was never completed. In June 1836 Théo wrote to the publisher Renduel as follows : 'Mr Eugène Renduel is urgently requested to have ready some money for the unfortunate Théophile Gautier who has dropped his in the river together with the newest of his three old hats. This accident has completely exhausted his means of subsistence. Gérard is also in the greatest misery and that is why he would like to sell you something very funny very dear because it is you. We shall write it together. It is the *Confessions of two gentlemen of Périgord*—it will certainly be a great success. You will give us each 600 francs, which is very reasonable for such a new and sublime idea. What do you say? We will pay homage to you this evening or tomorrow and contemplate in the depths of your office the radiant splendours of your editorial and dominatorial locks. May God preserve you from historical novels and the elder brother of the small-pox. Don't allow yourself to die without confession and above all without money.' The contract for this work was duly signed on 22 July, 1836 and in the following month, each armed with his advance of six hundred francs, the two friends set off together for Belgium.

They were oddly assorted companions, the lively and alert Théo darting his eyes from one window to the other of the coach whilst Gérard buried his nose in the *Nouvelle Héloise*. When travelling at night Gérard adopted a novel posture for sleeping which, as Théo says, most people would have employed for keeping awake. 'He knotted the two ends of a scarf to the roof of the carriage, passed his head through this sort of halter, and was soon drinking deep draughts from the black bowl of sleep. What surprised me very much was that he was not well and truly strangled;

apparently God, always fatherly, wished to spare him the penalty for having hanged himself.'

Their journey took them along the old Flanders road to Cambrai and Ostend. 'The sea is superb', wrote Théo to a friend, 'and we dabble in it every day. The women are not like the sea, far from it.' The women, indeed, were a disappointment to them. They had expected to find there the type of beauty they both admired, fair-haired and well-developed like some of Rubens's figures. Instead they found them dark-haired and thin. In Mons and Antwerp it was the same. Nevertheless, in the same letter Théo makes fun of his companion who, he says, 'is always in an alarming state of erection and walks with his lance in rest, as if he were going to play at quintain. . . . and gets himself turned out everywhere on account of his priapic tendencies.' As they wandered through the streets of the old cities, Gérard was always far ahead, walking with 'that peculiar wing movement which made him seem to walk by flying, or fly by walking, like the ostriches'. Théo, who moved more slowly, inspecting everything minutely, had no fear of losing his friend altogether, for he guarded the communal purse.

Before the end of their tour Gérard contracted a nervous fever which delayed them for some days in Belgium. On the way back he fell ill again at Presles. 'They applied leeches,' he wrote to his father from Passy where Théo took him to his father's house towards the end of September to recuperate. 'I have grown thinner, but now I am better.' Before the end of the month they were back in Paris.

During the days of his illness, Gérard had put the finishing touches to his comic opera, *Piquillo*, the forthcoming production of which had already been announced in the papers. Hippolyte Monpou, who had won popular acclaim for his work, had composed the music and with Dumas ostensibly as author the four-act piece seemed assured of success. The principal part of Sylvia was to be played by Mme Damoreau Cinthie, a singer of some repute. The two authors were to receive five thousand francs each on the first night, and to share one hundred and fifty francs for each subsequent performance. But there was an unexpected delay. *Piquillo* was not produced until the following year on the last day of October, and it was Jenny Colon who then took the part of Sylvia.

It has been suggested that some time during the interval Gérard paid his first visit to Germany, but there is no very clear evidence for this. After the abandonment of the Rue du Doyenné, he and Houssaye had joined Théo in the Rue Saint Germain des Prés. There they cooked for themselves, Houssaye being expert at making bread soup, Théo specializing in the preparation of macaroni and Gérard doing the shopping. Gérard slept very little. He was in the habit of reading late into the night by the light of a candle, the candlestick, to Théo's alarm, balanced precariously on his head.

He was still strongly under the influence of Hoffmann, whose tales led him into the realms of speculation on the supernatural. But he was an omnivorous and eclectic reader. If he modelled himself on Diderot, Rousseau and Sénancour, he was no less influenced by Sterne and Swift. Among his favourite books were the *Golden Ass* of Lucius Apuleius and Scarron's *Roman Comique*. He found a kindred spirit in Restif de la Bretonne. He could admire both Dante and Dickens. He was familiar with Pico de La Mirandola, Nicolas de Cusa, Court de Gebelin, Herbelot de Molainville, Swedenborg, and many abstruse and esoteric authors. But the book that most attracted him at this time was the *Hypnerotomachia Poliphili*.

Published in Latin in 1499, *The Dream of Poliphilus* by Francisco Colonna had first been translated into French in 1546. A modern adaptation had appeared in 1806. To Gérard, always alive to the possible significance of such resemblances, the name Colonna was inevitably connected with Jenny's surname, but it was the theme above all that appealed to him. Francisco falls in love with the beautiful Lucrezia Polia. She returns his love but because of her high birth they are prevented from marrying. They swear eternal fidelity to each other. Francisco becomes a monk, Lucrezia a nun. Each night they visit each other in dreams, and are finally united in mystical union beyond death. Gérard had already written for Jenny the slight and charming one-act play *Corilla* which was never produced but finally included in *Les Filles du Feu*. Its theme of mistaken identity clearly illustrates Gérard's obsession with resemblances. Now, the ideas he found in *Hypnerotomachia Poliphili* entirely engrossed him, and he set to work on the scenario of a drama based on Colonna's story, in which Jenny should play the part of Lucrezia Borgia.

As yet he had not met Jenny in person. Like Fabio in *Corilla*, he had adored in her 'only the actress, and his love required the distance and the glare of the footlights'. But now the dream was to spill over into life. Preparations for the production of *Piquillo* were already under way when Dumas and Méry, or some say Balzac, first introduced him to Jenny.

The real relationship between them ultimately presents a seemingly insoluble problem. Gérard never confided his most intimate thoughts and experiences even to his closest friends, and there are so many conflicting accounts of the affair that the true facts

remain a mater of conjecture. The only documents that survive are
the Letters to Jenny Colon. They are few in number and would
appear to have been written during the winter of 1837-1838.
Some of them were published in *Aurélia*, the two editors Gautier
and Houssaye presenting them as they had found them, without trying to co-ordinate them or restore their proper sequence, 'the
secret of which the poor dreamer carried with him'. A few others
were discovered later and in 1902 Victorien Sardou published
the whole series in a new order. Of Jenny's replies, apart from the
evidence implied in the letters themselves, no trace has survived.

The picture presented by them is that of a worldly woman,
already surrounded by admirers, bewildered but intrigued, flattered
but embarrassed by this new lover; now encouraging him with
slight favours, now fearful of a passion she could not understand
and which offered her glimpses of a completely alien world of
thought and emotion. He is both proud and humble. At one time
he tells her that he is 'a man of some consequence' or, remembering
his pretended descent from the knights of Otho's court, that he
is a 'descendant of a lord of a manor in Périgord'; he is 'an honourable man and in everything worthy of your choice'. At another time,
he apologizes for the 'momentary pride to which I gave way . . .
Ah! it was a laughable ambition that made me think I was so
close to a woman of your merit and beauty!' He reminds her that
'for a whole year I have been occupied in preparing a triumph
for you,' and then writes, 'A smile, a squeeze of the hand, a tender
word were worth a hundred times more than anything I have done.'

Throughout the course of the letters he is alternately elated and
depressed. Jenny does not altogether reject him, yet she is frightened by his passionate raptures and will not grant him the favours
she so liberally bestows on others. He has reason to believe that
she is 'not altogether indifferent' but she is 'so cruelly sensible, and
always so right'. He is too violent and at the same time too poetical
for the matter-of-fact Jenny. He writes:

You know that my sole happiness is to live and would be to die
for you. To die! O, God! Why does this idea keep recurring
on every occasion, as if death must be the price of the happiness
you promise me. Yet there is nothing gloomy for me in the
thought of Death; I picture her crowned with pale roses, as at
the end of a feast; I have sometimes dreamed that she awaited
me at the bedside of a woman I adored, not in the evening, but
in the morning after a night of intoxicating happiness, and that
she said to me 'Come, young man! You have had your night as
others have had their day! Now, come and sleep, come and rest

in my arms: there is nothing beautiful about me, but I am kind and comforting, and, though I do not offer pleasure, I give eternal peace!'

In another letter he writes:

Something recently has changed your attitude towards me, for you are too indulgent and too sensible really to take offence at a little roughness or a few follies, excusable surely in such a situation as mine. [He goes on to say that he believes some 'worthless and undeserving fellow, quite insignificant and frivolous' has been pestering her and ruining her reputation.] This is not a question of rivalry with me [but] If you would know how much I love and esteem you, there is one step I can take that will show you on whose arm you can rely. If I am mistaken in all my suppositions, reassure me, I beg you! Above all spare me the ridicule of committing myself with a man whom it would not in the least satisfy my vanity even to humiliate.

Evidently this letter was received with mockery, for he subsequently protests that 'a true passion is not to be trifled with' and warns her to 'beware, not of your heart, which is good, but of your disposition which is volatile and changeable. . . . As for jealousy, that side of my nature is quite dead.'

Acknowledging a change in his attitude to her, he writes:

Then it was not the woman in you that I loved; it was rather to the Divinity in you that I paid homage. Perhaps I ought always to have been contented with this humble role and not sought to persuade that beautiful idol whom, until then, I had adored at a distance, to descend from her pedestal. But am I to tell you that I have lost something of my illusion in seeing you so much nearer to me? No! . . . but in attaching itself to the reality, my love has changed its character.

That he was now under no illusion about her is clear when he writes 'What does it matter to me that you have belonged to others, that you belong to others now perhaps!' But then he pleads, somewhat illogically, that since she is the first woman he has ever loved, and since he is perhaps the first man who has been so much in love with her, that must constitute 'a sort of marriage in heaven'. While pursuing her as the object of physical desire, he still exalts her to the heights of a pure and mystical love after the pattern of Francisco Colonna's. This conflict leads to confusion, and he feels 'as if there were a circle of iron about my forehead'. Yet he feels that they 'are pledged to each other in life and in death'.

When she complains that he has wasted 'some hours' of her time, he rejoins that his love has wasted years of his life. At last, feeling that she is incapable of understanding the 'poetry and originality' of his love, he decides to admit the strength of his physical passion : 'I am forced to admit that my desire for you is as great as my love,' and he pleads 'for three years now I have been faithful to you. . . . If you have any feeling for me at all, you surely cannot abandon me again to those empty passions that destroy me.' Jenny relents. There is mention of her 'promise', but Gérard is still afraid of a mere 'cold compliance' on her part : 'I would rather never possess you at all than have in my arms a woman not won but merely resigned.' Finally she keeps her promise. 'That you would be as kind as you are beautiful, as tender as you are charming, ah ! that is what I never dared to hope.' In a state of profound emotional disturbance he bows his head, 'trembling as if beneath the breath of God'. Again he assures her that 'in the love between us there is something imperishable and divine.'

But almost immediately afterwards there is a rupture. He has earned her fierce resentment 'for some imprudence, perhaps, of which I may have been guilty but of which I am unaware even now. . . . Our poor honeymoon had scarcely completed its first quarter . . . and you know me so little still that you have neither understood me properly, nor judged me rightly.' He is still, he insists, her 'faithful and submissive friend, whose affection remains constant in spite of all bitter crosses', and he promises to preserve her good name by his discretion. His one consolation is to hope that, as she has once loved him, she must love him still. 'Thus I saw my Polia vanish at the instant when I thought to fold her in my arms,' Francisco Colonna had written in the *Hypnerotomachia,* and so Gérard's own dream dissolved. Jenny was 'for ever lost'.

Such in brief is the story of the letters. The problem is one of determining how authentically they reflect the true facts. That the letters were corrected and polished for eventual publication detracts nothing from their original validity. Gérard wrote out of his own experience. It was perfectly natural for him to make use in this way of a correspondence intimately expressive of emotions that had affected him so profoundly. One of the letters, considerably elaborated, formed the centrepiece of the story *Octavie,* a reminiscence of his visits to Italy. This, together with five others, had already appeared in an unsigned article as part of a proposed novel, in which they were supposed to have been written by one Dubourjet who had died in 1808 on his way to Santo Domingo. Later still Gérard had the idea of incorporating the whole series in a novel in letters about an adventurer named Brisacier, who pretended to claim descent from the royal family of Valois. But this project was eventually abandoned. It was evidently his final intention to include them in *Aurélia* and it was there at last that they found their true and proper setting.

That the letters are a genuine expression of real feelings is beyond question, but we do not even know whether Jenny actually received them all. Gautier speaks of the 'passionate and charming letters which he doubtless posted in his pocket, for she to whom they were addressed would surely have been moved by them', and he goes on to say that Gérard was so reserved that it was not known whether he had ever declared his love. Many years later, in conversation with Maxime du Camp, he told of a meeting with Jenny in Brussels when, speaking of Gérard, she declared 'I have only seen him once, when he came to offer me an opera, *The Queen of Sheba,* for which Meyerbeer was to write the music; I received bouquets, without knowing very well where they came from; I heard gossip about the affair in the theatre, but I didn't attach any importance to it. Don't accuse me of having caused him to suffer : when the one who loves is dumb, the one who is loved is deaf. Tell your friend Gérard de Nerval that I am innocent of the wrongs I am supposed to have committed.' According to Théo, when he told Gérard what she had said, the latter replied, 'What good would it have done if she had loved me', and he quoted from Heine, 'He who loves without hope a second time is a madman. I am that madman. The sky, the sun, the stars laugh at it; I, too, laugh at it; I laugh at it and am dying of it.' By the time of the meeting in Brussels Jenny would already have been married and Gérard would have been under treatment for his first mental illness. It would therefore have been quite natural for her to do her best to conceal any intimacy there might once have been between them. We must presume that at the time of the production of *Piquillo* Gérard must have known Jenny and that, coming into close contact with her as he would have done, he could hardly have refrained from declaring his love for her. There is no reason to think that they did not exchange letters. Gérard himself tells us in *Aurélia* that he destroyed Jenny's letters after her death.

Whatever the truth behind the courtship described in Gérard's letters to Jenny, the fact is that little more than a month after their estrangement, on 11 April 1838, Jenny married a member of the orchestra of the Opéra Comique, Louis Marie Gabriel Leplus, a flautist and organizer of theatrical tours, who had long been her suitor.

The various and contradictory accounts of Jenny's surrender and

of the subsequent rupture between the lovers afford no very con-
clusive evidence. Georges Bell – his real name was Joachim Hounau
– who, though nineteen years his junior, was one of Gérard's
closest and most loyal friends during the last years of his life and
who later acted as Méry's secretary, relates a story which he
claims to have heard from Méry himself, of a dinner given by
Gérard for his friends. Jenny, who was also of the party, was in a
particularly lively mood. Towards the end of the dinner they were
all a little intoxicated. Suddenly Jenny rose and 'taking Gérard by
the arm drew him away into the realm of fantasy.' The curtains
of the famous bed closed around them, and the lovers' ecstasies
were accompanied by the sound of laughter, song, and the merry
clink of glasses.

The Gérard of this story is quite out of character. It is hard to
believe that this man, normally shy and reserved in the extreme,
could ever have behaved publicly in this way, especially with the
woman who was the divinity he worshipped. Moreover Bell's
statement that Gérard himself confirmed the truth of the story is
in flagrant contradiction to his previous emphasis on Gérard's
reticence on the subject of his relations with Jenny. Then, too,
the days of the Rue du Doyenné were over before Gérard met
Jenny for the first time. Méry, whose descriptions of the East were
so vivid and colourful as to convince most of his readers that he
had travelled widely although actually he had never left home,
was a great fantasist, and in all probability the story was a figment
of his imagination.

According to Alphonse Karr it was Dumas who undertook to
arrange matters for Gérard, but the lovers came together in the
sordid surroundings of a hotel room and Gérard, who had dreamed
of an exquisite setting for their union, was totally disillusioned.
That he was the victim of his own sensitivity may well be true
and would account not only for his increasingly obsessive feeling
of guilt for an offence which, though committed involuntarily, demanded expiation, but also for his constant preoccupation later with
the fear of impotence.

Georges Bell, on the other hand, gives quite a different account
of the rupture. One day, he says, the musician Zimmermann was
giving a brilliant entertainment at his house to which for some
whimsical reason actresses were invited only if they were married.
Jenny was thus excluded. In desperation she came to Gérard, suggesting that he should marry her. Taken by surprise, he hesitated
and demanded time for consideration; this was the offence that
caused the breach.

Arsène Houssaye too has his own version, according to which

Gérard went to visit Jenny one day, carrying a bunch of flowers. Entering the room he seized her round the waist and ardently pressed his lips to the nape of her neck. Startled by his abruptness, Jenny instinctively repulsed him. Gérard stepped back awkwardly, bumped into a table, and overturned a valuable Sèvres coffee set, a present to Jenny from the Duke of Orleans. And it was for this incident that he was never to be forgiven.

Whatever the cause of the estrangement, Gérard felt that it had been foredoomed.

'I would not attach too much importance to presentiments,'[1] he wrote in *Aurélia*; 'chance gives rise to strange coincidences; but at the time I was preoccupied with our too fleeting union. I had given her a ring of unique workmanship, the jewel of which was an opal shaped like a heart. As this ring was too big for her finger, I had had the fatal idea of having it cut to reduce the circle; it was only when I heard the sound of the saw that I realized my mistake. I seemed to see the blood flowing.'

He was to see Jenny once again two years later in Brussels and to believe that he read forgiveness in her eyes, but when she died in 1842 he felt 'only a vague sorrow mixed with hope', for by then Adrienne-Jenny had undergone a further transformation; she was Aurélia, the mystical divine lover and protectress who belonged to him more in death than in life.

The symbolic significance of the name Aurélia, by which he chose to designate her, is clear. In Hoffmann's tale, *The Vampire*, Aurélia is the vampire wife of a young count who, when he discovers her dreadful secret, is destroyed by her. Gérard felt that his life had been destroyed by his love for Jenny. Yet he remained faithful to her 'after his fashion', pursuing always the same woman under different guises. As Colonna had written in the *Hypnerotomachia*, 'it is she whom you see, but if you can have been deceived, if it is another beauty who has taken her lineaments and

---

[1] Yet in *Un Tour dans le Nord*, recounting his travels in England and Flanders, with reference to a railway accident in which sixteen people were killed and many seriously injured, he relates how, 'I had reached the station and was ready to take my seat in the train when some intuition, I don't know what, some hidden *genius*, suddenly made me change my mind. There was something sinister about the whistle for departure; the inspector who pointed out to me the booking-office looked like a vampire; the procession of passengers I caught sight of through the doors reminded me of processions of quite another kind. . . . In that I was a little mistaken, for it was the day before the accident that this happened; but remember that I had decided to stop off for a day in Amiens, and that, consequently, I would have taken the fatal train on the next day in order to get to Antwerp. In fact I always feel more comfortable in obeying presentiments.'

her stature in order to seduce you, you yield to your misfortune, you become inconstant and forsworn. Forgive me, Polia, and realize that in seeking you always it is still you I love, even though I may seem to you unfaithful.'

But with Jenny's death, the disinherited Gérard, 'widowed, disconsolate', was to enter a new phase, still following his 'one star' into esoteric regions of dream and fantasy where, after his descent into hell, he was to be rewarded with a beatific vision which nevertheless had no power to sustain him in a world of harsh realities.

6

Germany

Gérard's immediate reaction was to seek distraction in work and travel. The two could be conveniently combined. The money he had received for *Piquillo* had enabled him to pay off some of his debts, so that for the moment he found himself less hard-pressed. Moreover his collaboration with Dumas gave promise of continuing success. They were already engaged on two new projects, *l'Alchimiste* and *Léo Burckart*. The latter was Gérard's special care. This was to be the play signed, according to their agreement, by himself alone, as Dumas had already been acknowledged as the author of *Piquillo*. Dumas's hand in it was in fact confined to 'the dramatic arrangement of the scenes and the execution of the dialogue'. It was throughout entirely Gérard's inspiration. Both works were well under way, and *Léo Burckart* was sufficiently advanced to obtain for Gérard an advance of 1,200 francs from the director, Harel. The play was based on the stabbing, for political reasons, of the German playwright Kotzebue at Weimar in 1761. *L'Alchimiste,* on which Dumas was more specifically engaged, was a free adaptation from the German. It was therefore decided to finish the work in Germany, where they could obtain more documentary information about the murder of Kotzebue and where Gérard could improve his knowledge of the language for, as he wrote in a letter to his father during this visit, 'I still have difficulty in translating or understanding certain things.'

Gérard was to travel direct. Dumas, who wanted first to visit Belgium, was to write to him when he arrived in Germany arranging a meeting-place. In due course the letter arrived :

Dear friend, out of consideration for you, I have chosen, for the hatching of the egg which you have laid, Frankfurt-on-Maine, our Goethe's birthplace : come and join me and may the shade of the author of *Werther* watch over you during the journey. Although the town is not large and I am not difficult to find, get it well into your head that I am staying at the Roman Emperor Hotel. It takes five days to get here, taking plenty of

time by the way, try not to take more than fifteen. I am not
worried about you, pecuniarily speaking. I understand from
Harel that he has just paid you twelve hundred francs; even
supposing he may have misrepresented the amount and it is
only half what he says, you must have six hundred francs; I
know your way of travelling; with six hundred francs, you would
make a tour of the world.

Gérard's way of travelling, as Dumas well knew, was apt to be
erratic. 'I love to depend a little on chance,' he wrote to a friend;
'the numbered preciseness of railway stops, the punctuality of
steamships, arriving at a fixed hour and day, do not much please a
poet.' Elsewhere he says, 'What I like more than anything else in
travelling is to breathe the air of forests and plains . . . to wander
about the twisting streets of towns, mingling with the variegated
crowd which buzzes with a strange language, and for a day to
be a part of its never-ending life, a curious test and a salutary
isolation for the man who knows how to escape sometimes from
the mild constraints of habit.' His journey on this occasion was
typical in its vicissitudes. From the beginning everything seemed to
go wrong. Answering Dumas's letter before his departure, he wrote,
'I did in fact receive twelve hundred francs . . . from Harel.
These twelve hundred francs have been somewhat reduced by
your fault, because you delayed for two days to tell me where I
should join you. In two days much water flows under the bridges
and a good many gold coins through the meshes of a purse.
Never mind, I am leaving, now that I have received my letter,
expect me any day.'
What actually happened was that Gérard found in an antique
shop a fine sixteenth-century bed which he could not resist buying.
Unfortunately he had nowhere to put it; so it was arranged that
the dealer should store it for him – at a price. Then there was a
magnificent chest which had belonged to Diane de Poitiers. It was
an opportunity not to be missed. One purchase led to another, and
Gérard finally left the shop having acquired a whole roomful of
treasures, but with only one hundred and eighty of the twelve
hundred francs left in his pocket.
Having made up his mind to start for Germany that same day,
he next went to book his seat in the diligence which was due to
leave the Rue Notre Dame des Victoires at eight o'clock in the
evening. There was only an outside place left and, realizing that he
would have a cold journey, he decided to buy an overcoat. This
cost him a further forty-five francs. But it was not to be the last
of his expenses before leaving. Quite by chance he happened to

meet Théo and a friend. The three dined together in celebration of Gérard's departure, and it was naturally Gérard who paid the bill – fifteen francs each. Afterwards they took coffee in the garden of the Palais Royal, which was quite near the Rue Notre Dame des Victoires. At half past seven Gérard suddenly remembered that he had left his bundle of clothes for the journey on a chair in his bedroom. He called a porter, gave him a written order for the bundle and promised to pay him double if he could bring it to the diligence in time. At a quarter to eight they went to the coach station where they anxiously awaited the porter's arrival, but there was no sign of him. Eight o'clock struck. Gérard said good-bye to his friends and took his seat. At a crack of the whip the coach was in motion, the horses setting off at a good round trot. Suddenly there were cries from the street. The porter appeared, breathless and exhausted, holding on high the forgotten bundle. But once under way, nothing could persuade the coachman to stop. Philosophically Gérard reflected that a change of clothes was not essential and that all he would need on the journey was a new shirt. This he eventually bought at Nancy, and it cost him another ten francs.

By the time he reached Strasbourg he had only twenty-seven francs left and after spending three days at the Raven Hotel he was one franc short when it came to paying the bill. The hotel-keeper obligingly waived the difference. Upon enquiry Gérard learned that the cost of the journey to Frankfurt by boat was twenty-seven francs. His one recourse was to pawn his overcoat, but it fetched no more than seven francs. Undeterred he set off for Baden Baden on foot. There he installed himself comfortably at the Sun Hotel, and immediately wrote to Dumas : 'a number of circumstances, some more pressing than others, keep me in Baden Baden; the latest of all, but the one I place first so as not to tire you with a recital of the others, is that I have no more money. So send me what you can poste restante at Strasbourg, and send me your letter of advice in duplicate. One to the Raven Hotel at Strasbourg. The other to the Sun Hotel at Baden. The very day I receive your reply, I will leave for Frankfurt.'

After some days he received the reply : 'My dear Gérard, if by chance you receive this letter at Baden Baden go straight away to Strasbourg; in a letter addressed to you at the Raven Hotel you will find a bill of exchange for a hundred and fifty francs, underwritten by Mr Eloi, director of the coach service. As I hope that nothing will interfere with your departure, I shall expect you on Monday or Tuesday next.' Gérard immediately set out for Strasbourg. The letter was awaiting him at the Raven, together with the bill of exchange, but when he presented this to Mr Elgé, on whom it was drawn, it appeared that Mr Eloi had been presuming on his father's business connection with Mr Elgé, and, because there had lately been some disagreement between father and son, Mr Elgé refused to honour the bill. With one franc only in his pocket Gérard returned to the Raven to dine frugally on a plate of soup, pretending that he had a weak stomach and could not digest anything more solid. Then he set off again for Baden Baden.

'O Dumas,' he wrote to his friend, explaining his situation, 'there is some fatality in everything that happens to me.' His baggage had arrived, but he could not collect it for lack of the eighteen francs that were due on it. Nevertheless with characteristic optimism he decided that sooner or later the money would arrive. 'As to that I have no doubt and I am going to sleep on several pillows . . . the Sun Hotel is hospitable, I shall dine and sleep with confidence.' To pass the intervening time he set out with only a few sous in his pocket on an excursion on foot through the Black Forest. At last the money from Frankfurt reached him, and he was able to pay off his hotel bill, collect his luggage and rejoin his friend. After a short stop at Mannheim he travelled up the Rhine as far as Mayence and, continuing thence by coach, arrived in Frankfurt on 16 September, having occupied twenty-nine days on the journey that Dumas had told him could be made comfortably in five.

They began work together without delay, but there were many distractions. Gérard wrote to his father,

> We are settled in a little house which he (Dumas) has rented until the end of the month, and surrounded by the attentions and friendship of the whole town. They give us parties, suppers, excursions, to such an extent that it is impossible to accept a quarter of the invitations and we can scarcely work except at night. . . . The evening before last we had an evening and supper at the Russian envoy's. Yesterday Mr Charles Durand, the director of the *Frankfurt Journal*, took us driving all day in his carriage in the country round about; we dined at Homburg and took coffee in one of the two French villages inhabited by the refugees from the Edict of Nantes. This evening we go to the theatre, in the Rothschilds' box, who have invited us. They have also organized a hunting party for the day after tomorrow, but I do not know if we shall go, as Dumas is not very well. It is amazing to find how highly French literary people are thought of and how well received they are in Germany.

There were also excursions, for documentary purposes, to the scenes of the drama on which Gérard was engaged. The two friends and collaborators went to Mannheim and Heidelberg. They visited the cemetery and the place of execution of the young student, Karl Sand, who had murdered Kotzebue in 1819. They interviewed the governor of the prison in which he had been confined, and Dr Widmann, the executioner, at Mannheim.

> There we were, knocking at the executioner's door. After ten minutes we heard a noise of spurred heels, then many bolts were drawn and the door was opened. A very young man, of a rather stocky figure and with a romantic face, asked us what we wanted, without inviting us inside. We told him we were writers and were collecting information on Karl Sand. Then he threw open the door and showed us into a very bright room on the ground floor, asking us to wait while he shut the heavy door again, which he did with some care.

After some general conversation Dr Widmann supplied them with the information they required and showed them the sword his father had used.

> Until then we had imagined that the head was removed quite simply with a good stroke of a dragoon's sabre or a scimitar like the Turks' and the weapon that we were looking at quite confounded our ideas. The inner side of the cutting edge was like that of a pruning knife; moreover the blade was hollow and contained quicksilver so that when the sword struck, this metal, flowing towards the point, rendered the stroke more certain. Thus the whole of the doctor's art consisted in effecting a rotatory movement round the neck which, before touching the bone, took away nearly all the flesh; so the head is not chopped off but, so to speak, culled. We were contented with the explanation, without asking for experience.
>
> Moreover, our poor executioner from Baden has never exercised his father's terrible calling. He even confided to us that he trembled every day lest anyone should commit a crime in the duchy, fortunately a very rare occurrence, and that he would not very well know what to do in such a case.

They returned to Paris at the beginning of October to arrange for the production of the two dramas. *Léo Burckart* was to be presented at the Rennaissance Theatre which was opened by Antenor Joly in November with a revival of *Ruy Blas,* but owing to the success of the latter the authors agreed not to insist on the fulfilment of their contract, and it was finally *l'Alchimiste* that was presented there on 10 April 1839.

C

Meanwhile, in March, Gérard completely revised *Léo Burckart,* which Harel eventually produced at the Porte Saint Martin. *L'Alchimiste* had a fair success, and Gérard's share of the profits was twelve hundred francs, exactly the amount already advanced by Harel. But it was on *Léo Burckart* that Gérard had pinned all his hopes of improving not only his financial position but also his literary reputation. He had put a great deal of himself into the play, and particularly into the character of Franz Lewald.

Franz is just such a product of the age as Gérard, that age which 'began amidst storm and fire. War roared around our cradles. . . . Now that a flat calm has succeeded so many stormy tempests, is it any wonder that we have difficulty in recovering from our premature efforts, and that we have nothing to offer women but a spirit blighted before its time, and passions already enervated by doubt and misfortunes?' Before leaving Frankfurt for a time, Franz was in love with Marguerite. When he returns he finds she is married to Léo Burckart, a progressive journalist who has been appointed prime minister. On coming to power Burckart finds himself forced to sacrifice his love of liberty in the cause of maintaining the law. He is consequently regarded as a traitor by the students and when they protest against his oppression in vain, one of their secret societies to which Franz belongs plans to assassinate him. The instrument of the murder is chosen by lot in secret tribunal and the lot falls to Franz, but he recoils from the deed and, having confessed his love to Marguerite, kills himself instead. Burckart, believing the safety of his home to be threatened, relinquishes power and so preserves his domestic happiness.

The play was dogged by ill luck from the beginning. A copy had been submitted to the board of censors in November, and owing to the fact that it presented the dark practices of secret societies and political assassination 'in the most lively and spirited colours' it was deemed that it would work 'strongly on the imagination and would give rise to the most dangerous impressions'. At the same time it was recognized that the harmfulness of the play lay 'more in the actual spectacle than in the political ideas of which it treats'. Finally after a long delay it was passed, but the season was already well advanced when Harel was at last able to produce it. Moreover the economies he was forced to make through lack of funds not only involved the exclusion of whole scenes and much consequent rewriting but left much to be desired in the production. The net result was that the play survived no more than thirty performances.

Apart from an indemnity of six hundred francs granted by the censor for the delay in its production, Gérard gained nothing.

Disappointed and once again in financial difficulties he fell into deep depression. But as further compensation he was entrusted with a mission to report on the question of copyright in Germany and Austria. This afforded him the opportunity of travelling again, and to the countries of his choice. From the time of his earliest acquaintance with its literature Germany had attracted him, the 'land of Goethe and Schiller, the old Germany, mother of us all – Teutonia'. Inevitably, too, for him it evoked thoughts of his mother, who lay buried there. On his previous visit he had found the people extremely hospitable and, despite his still defective knowledge of the language, he could feel as much at home there as anywhere. Then, too, he had determined to visit Vienna, where he had been promised various introductions, including one to M. de Metternich which would ensure his acceptance in the best society.

The journey would necessitate the usual strict economy and part of it would be made on foot. This he had in mind when, calling one evening on his friend Edouard Ourliac, his eyes fell on a pair of boots in much better condition than his own. 'I saw with pleasure', he wrote to him later, 'that your boots would replace mine to advantage; so I put them on.' Thus equipped, he set off light-heartedly on 31 October for Lyon, having determined first to visit Switzerland.

7

Vienna

Gérard scarcely knew himself where his journey might eventually take him. His object was simply to visit countries which he had not yet seen. For a moment he thought of returning to Italy, but he was quite content to be guided by necessity. 'At this season,' he wrote in his account of the journey in the introduction to the *Voyage en Orient,* 'one has hardly any choice of routes; one has to take the one that has not been invaded by snow or floods or robbers.' He preferred to travel haphazardly. He felt that if he set out, fully equipped, on a carefully planned journey, he would find nothing to write about, and it was only by means of the articles he could sell to various periodicals that he could defray his expenses. 'Imagine', he says, 'the imprudence of a traveller who, too capricious to take the railways, almost direct, surrenders himself to all the hazards of the diligences!' It was, in fact, exactly these hazards that fed his zest for travelling, and he goes on to give an account of his journey very much in the manner of his acknowledged master, Sterne.

From Macon he went to Bourg with the intention of taking the coach on to Geneva. But on arriving in Bourg at eight o'clock in the evening he found that there was no direct coach service to Geneva, and he was faced with the choice of either making a long detour through Lyon or going to Pont d'Ain to pick up the coach from Lyon, thereby saving ten hours' journey. Accordingly he took the coach from Bourg at eleven o'clock. At three o'clock in the morning he was set down on the main road from Lyon with his baggage at his feet. It was drizzling, the road was in darkness and he could see no houses and no light. He was told to follow the road for a kilometre and a half and he would find an inn where he could take shelter if everyone was not asleep. The coach went on to Lyon and Gérard, taking up his bags, began walking. After knocking at the door of the inn for an hour he managed to wake somebody and, once inside, all his troubles were forgotten. 'The inn at Pont d'Ain is an inn of Cockaigne. Coming down in the morning I found myself in a huge and grand kitchen. Fowls were turning on the spits, fish were cooking on the stoves. A very animated company of hunters was gathered round a well-furnished table. The host was a fat man and the hostess a strong woman, both very kindly.'

But the Geneva coach, he learned, would not be passing until two o'clock next day. There was the mail, however, which would be going through at ten o'clock in the evening. It duly arrived, and while the driver was having supper, Gérard was taken out to the coach-house to be shown his place.

Oh! Surprise! It was a basket.

Yes, a simple basket slung on an old carriage-frame, fine for containing letters and packages; but the traveller got into it just like a parcel.

A young lady in mourning and in tears had arrived from Grenoble in this incredible vehicle; I had to take my place at her side. The impossibility of retaining a fixed position among the packages perforce mingled our destinies: the lady ended up by drying her tears which were due to the death of an uncle in Grenoble. She was returning to Ferney, where her family lived.

We talked a great deal about Voltaire. We went along slowly because of the continual rises and descents. The driver, too scornful of his carriage to take a place in it himself, whipped his horse from down below when every now and then it skirted the edge of a precipice.

The Rhone flowed on our right, some hundreds of feet below the road. . . .

From time to time we stopped for a moment in little towns, in villages where we heard nothing but the cries of animals awakened by our passage. The driver threw packages to invisible hands or paws, and then we left again with his little horse at full trot.

Towards dawn we saw, from the top of the mountains, a great sheet of water, wide and reaching to the distant horizon like a sea. It was Lake Leman.

An hour later we were taking coffee at Ferney while waiting for the omnibus to Geneva.

From there, in two hours' journey between fields still green, through a charming countryside, among gardens and cheerful villas, I arrived in the country of Jean Jacques Rousseau.

He spent two days at Geneva, and two in Berne, 'surely the most beautiful town in all Switzerland'. He relates how at Constance he made the acquaintance of a pretty young Englishwoman. At a table d'hôte her husband, who was in poor health and had been ordered by his doctors not to drink, insisted on ordering champagne. The young wife was unable to dissuade him but when the bottle was produced she offered it round the table. The husband promptly ordered more. Again she offered it round. Gérard, sympathizing with her predicament, did his best to help her by drinking glass after glass until the husband, angry at having scarcely been given a chance to taste the wine and jealous of the attentions paid to Gérard by his wife, rose and left the table.

The anecdote was first recounted in a letter to his friends in 1834 as having taken place at Marseilles. The pretty young Englishwoman clearly made a strong impression on him, and she was to provide the model, in his final version of the story, for Octavie, so jealously watched by her paralytic husband that he would not allow her out of his sight.

Approaching Constance down the mountain gorges of the canton of Zurich, Gérard had first caught sight of the lake in the distance at sunset, and had admired its wonderful situation, 'like an Istanbul of the West', but he did not stay there. He was afraid to examine it too closely for fear that the reality would not match his imagined impression of it, and he hurried away before daylight. Already he was beginning to experience the disillusion of many travellers and to find that, in Stevenson's words, 'to travel hopefully is a better thing than to arrive'. 'It is a sad experience,' he writes, 'as one travels further, to lose, town by town and country by country, all that beautiful universe which one created for oneself when young, through books and pictures and dreams. The world thus imagined by children is so rich, so beautiful, that one cannot tell whether it is an exaggerated notion of inculcated ideas or a recollection of a previous existence and the magical geography of an unknown planet.'

Even so, he had an ever-increasing longing to visit the Orient, whose constant appeal rested not only in its exotic and romantic associations, but also in its being the original source of those esoteric arts and religions which had interested him since the days of his childish explorations in his uncle Boucher's library. When at length, by way of Augsburg, Munich, Salzburg and Linz, he arrived in Vienna on 19 November, he dreamed of continuing his journey later, if he could obtain enough money, to Constantinople. At the end of his stay he was to write, 'In Vienna, this winter, I have lived in a continuous dream. Is it already the delicious atmosphere of the Orient wafting about my head and heart? – And here I am only halfway there.'

He remained in Vienna for a little more than three months.

During that time he applied himself conscientiously to the task of his mission, but he was also determined to enjoy himself. Vienna was traditionally the city of gaiety and pleasure, and he was eager to sample all its delights. At that time in 1840 Philibert Audebrand recalled, 'Gérard still possessed a youthful appearance and the chivalrous manners displayed by the generation of 1830. He wore a chestnut goatee which made him look like a Van Dyck portrait. His slightly emaciated face was animated by a look full of fire and touched with a little mischief. Of medium height, rather slightly built without being thin, he was dressed, as at that period became a writer already attended by success, not too elegantly, but not with too much negligence either.'

In search of distraction, he frequented all the places of popular entertainment, as he had done in Paris : theatres, taverns and balls. Following Byron's advice to travellers in *Don Juan*, he looked for 'some pretty young person of the town who would be willing to help me towards a familiarity with the current idiom'. One evening at the Leopoldstadt theatre he fell in with a charming young blonde who was waiting for her mistress to arrive. 'Imagine,' he wrote enthusiastically in a letter to Théo, 'she is one of those beauties of whom we have so often dreamed. . . . Picture to yourself a ravishing blonde head, an incredibly white skin that might have been preserved under glass; the noblest features; an aquiline nose, a high forehead, cherry-red lips; a full, plump pigeon neck encircled with a necklace of pearls; firm white shoulders displaying the strength of Hercules and the weakness and charm of a two-year-old child.' The familiar traits are immediately recognizable. Katty is another Adrienne or Jenny. Before long she went away to Brunn to visit her sick mother. Meanwhile Gérard met in the Prater another charming blonde, Vahby. No doubt it was one of these to whom his friend Weill refers when he says, 'It was in Vienna that, for the first and last time, I ever saw Gérard with a mistress. She was a Hungarian.' And he adds. 'It was delightful to see the elegant Gérard beside his charmer, at the Karl theatre, crunching a small sausage seasoned with horseradish which he drew out of a white paper cornet and which he crammed between the white teeth of his adored.'

Such ephemeral and easy liaisons, however, with which Gérard reproached himself in later years, would seem not to have been so uncommon if we are to believe Arsène Houssaye. He relates how, some days after a lunch to which Gérard had invited him together with a young woman – 'a very imperfect dove with feathers damaged by the wind', – when he asked news of her, Gérard replied, 'Oh, how glad we were to be rid of each other.' And on another occasion at Versailles Gérard introduced him to a beauty of opulent proportions whom he was consoling for the departure of her soldier lover. 'He had so well tamed this athletic nymph that she had a blind admiration for her poet, reading his books all day and singing the old songs of Valois which he had taught her. "If it hadn't been for her expanse of wing," said Gérard, "I should have taken her off to Montmartre to live alone with her." '

Gérard had met Alexandre Weill, a journalist, poet and dramatist and the author of various occult works, when he had been staying in Frankfurt with Dumas two years before. He had then persuaded Weill to go to Paris to try his luck. There he had introduced him to Hugo, Balzac, Méry, Emile de Girardin, Théophile Gautier, Cassagnac, Texier, Musset, Philarète Chasles, Royer, Sue, and at the Divan Lepelletier, a café which was at that time the meeting place of Parisian literary and artistic circles. In return Weill exerted considerable influence in fostering Gérard's close friendship with Heine. Weill remained one of Gérard's most faithful friends until the end of his life. During the winter of 1839-40 he too was in Vienna, as confidential secretary to Charles Beriot, the celebrated Belgian violinist, who was giving a series of recitals there. It was Weill who introduced Gérard to Saphir, the editor of the *Theater Zeitung*. Saphir invited them to dinner and 'it was in this way', writes Gérard, 'that I became a contributor to the theatrical journal of Vienna. I hurried off to a café and at midnight I had finished the first of a series of studies on French literature. The next day, at the editorial office, I was paid ten florins.'

It was by such means, combined with his contributions to the Paris journals, that he was managing precariously to live. As early as 26 November 1839, he was writing to his father in desperation for some assistance. 'Now I have to make a demand which requires some explanation.' It would seem simple enough, he said, in the ordinary course of events to borrow two hundred francs from a father when one is in need, but he had for several years made a point of supporting himself entirely. Now he was down to his last one hundred and forty francs. There were necessary expenses : his hotel, some indispensable books, lessons in German (the pronunciation of which still created great difficulties for him), shoes, gloves, a white tie, in order to make himself presentable in the evenings. In a month's time, or two at most, he was to receive a further four hundred francs. Formerly his father had allowed him four hundred francs a year, but for the past four years he had received nothing and had not asked for anything even when he had previously been in great straits. He would pay off the loan at the rate of fifty francs a month.

It was a long and carefully worded letter, but it evoked no response from Dr Labrunie beyond reproaches and accusations directed against Gérard's friends for having led him astray. The injustice of these accusations roused Gérard and for once he adopted a less conciliatory attitude in their defence. In a letter dated 30 January he wrote:

As to your writing to me that my friends are in some sort responsible, I will tell you that none of my friends approved my enterprise and that they all advised me to stick to writing, which I should have done if my relatives' continual fears for my future had not made me myself nervous about my future means of existence, and it was this that unhappily led me to attempt a speculation in publishing instead of writing. . . . I am amazed to see you accuse my friends, who had nothing to do with these troubles, and who are simply my literary colleagues who have all rendered me service by encouraging me to work and have helped me on occasion. My friends are well enough known; there is Théophile who has enabled me to earn 250 francs a month for two years, by making me collaborator in his column in *La Presse*, and who introduced me to M. Lingay, to whom I owe my mission; there is Alphonse Karr, who has enabled me to earn 400 francs a month from *Figaro* which he edits; there is M. Victor Hugo who has been useful to me ten times, has introduced me to two periodicals, and has, besides, recently shared in soliciting the minister in my favour. There is Alexandre Dumas, who enabled me to earn 6,000 francs by *Piquillo* which helped me to pay off part of what I owed, and since then 1,200 francs by *l'Alchimiste*.

Since Dr Labrunie remained inflexible, Gérard was forced to make the most of his own slender resources. Circumstances were not made any easier at first by the censorship. One day he found that he was being followed in his peregrinations about the city. When he tackled his shadow, 'the poor man appeared very embarrassed; I put him at his ease, telling him that I knew that the Viennese police were obliged to keep an eye on foreigners, and particularly the French; tomorrow, I added, I will go and see your superior and reassure him about my intentions.' He was politely received by the chief of police, who told him that he had been greatly amused by the adventures Gérard had recounted in his letters to his friends. 'So you have been reading them?' Gérard enquired. 'Oh, don't worry,' was the reply, 'there is nothing compromising in your correspondence. The government rather appreciates those foreigners who, far from fomenting intrigues, wholeheartedly enjoy the pleasures afforded by the good city of Vienna.'

'He ended by asking me to come whenever I liked to read him the papers which were in opposition to the police . . . it being understood that this was the most liberal place in the Empire. . . . One could talk about anything there without danger.'

After this Gérard was free to wander as he pleased about the city. In the central square he found a shop-sign, a portrait of the archduchess Sophie, which immediately reminded him of 'the Other, dream of my young love . . . Diana of Valois'. He was still involved in his vision of an ideal love, from which more mundane contacts could never distract him: the baroness de Feuchères still rode through the woods in his imagination.

Christmas was a time of religious celebration and of general festivity, a combination which he found profoundly exciting. People went straight from church to the balls. There were decorated Christmas trees everywhere. 'The interiors of the churches, above all of St Etienne, were magnificent and radiant. What I admired most was not only the huge crowd in festive costumes, the silver altar sparkling in the centre of the choir, the hundreds of musicians suspended, so to speak, in the slender balconies that extended along the whole length of the pillars, but that frank and sincere faith that united all the voices in a marvellous hymn.' In his childhood it had been the musical voices of his young companions that had enchanted him, and now it was in music that he found his greatest satisfaction. Vienna was the city of music. Composers and performers flocked to it to such an extent that the French ambassador made fun of the 'encumbrance of pianos'. Gérard had every opportunity of hearing the best. He was well received in the highest circles of society. The French ambassador, M. de Sainte Aulaire, who had also produced a translation of *Faust*, made much of him. Among the regular guests at the embassy were the princes Schwartzenberg, Esterhazy, Dietrichstein, Field-marshal Mormont, the Duke of Ragusa, and M. de Metternich. When there was not a ball, the evenings were passed in reading comedies or in playing proverbs or charades.

Perhaps it was at the ambassador's table that he came face to face with the fair archduchess whose portrait on the shop-sign he had already admired, but who was to remain an inaccessible vision, to be exalted into the hierarchy of his divine and spiritual loves. Certainly it was at the embassy that he met the enchanting Marie Pleyel, the celebrated pianist who, having been fêted in St Petersburg, was now making a tour of Europe with an orchestra conducted by Mendelssohn. In Vienna it was Liszt who conducted her to the piano. The wife of a piano-maker from Strasbourg and only three years older than Gérard, she was beautiful and talented.

Slim and dark-haired, she in no way corresponded to Gérard's ideal of feminine beauty, but in what purports to be a translation of an article by Saphir, he describes 'a pair of eyes which are the twilight of a spring evening in the Alhambra, a radiant face like the pale reflection of the moon, a voice that sounds like the passionate strain of an andante, and a smile that would seem to be the dream of a love poem.' She was a friend of Jules Janin and having been introduced to her Gérard wrote in a letter to Janin, 'Mme Pleyel was only interested in you, and in me by consequence.' He gives an ironic, but nevertheless true, picture of himself on this occasion: 'Your friend has dined comfortably; he has drunk French and Hungarian wines; has taken coffee and a liqueur; he is well-dressed, his linen is exquisitely fine, his hair silky and very slightly waved . . . it is generally agreed that he is a charming conversationalist. He does not talk much; but when he is warmed up, he talks well.'

Gérard was easily won over by Marie's charm and her romantic, Spanish type of beauty. Delighted to find that he was capable of falling in love again, he wrote her an effusive letter, employing many of the terms and phrases he had previously used in his letters to Jenny. Immediately after posting it, he began to regret his impetuosity. On reflection, the letter seemed to him a profanation of his former love. When he met Marie again the next evening she expressed surprise at the passionate tone of his letter which had seemed to her to range over the whole gamut of a lover's emotions. Gérard, already aware that his sudden enthusiasm had carried him beyond the bounds of discretion, confessed that he had misinterpreted his own feelings and humbly begged her forgiveness for having unintentionally deceived her.

Such is the account of the affair that Gérard gives in *Aurélia*. Is there any need to question it? Marie Pleyel, it would seem, was of an extremely sympathetic nature, Perhaps she was initially offended by his odd behaviour, but she would not have harboured a grievance against anyone; moreover she was probably as susceptible to his charm as all the rest of his acquaintance. That they remained on good terms is shown by a letter written by her the following May to Jules Janin, in which she enquires, 'What is that nice little Gérard doing, who was so fond of you? I have a great friendship for that sweet poet whose soul is incapable of dreaming any unkindness.' Gérard himself gives two other versions of the story, one in the introduction to the *Voyage en Orient,* which may be regarded as a somewhat fanciful account to entertain his readers, the other, in *La Pandora*, a seemingly distorted account written during a period of mental stress, which is remarkable for the animosity and resentment displayed towards the protagonist.

The plausible and well-documented thesis of L. H. Sebillotte,[1] according to which the disasters attending Gérard's love affairs were due to a partial or intermittent impotence, is not necessary to explain his tragedy. Sebillotte stresses the psychological origin of the supposed defect, and certainly if there was any such impediment to his love, it would seem to have been purely psychological. The trouble was that the essential duality of his nature compelled him more and more to dissociate physical from spiritual love.

A clue to his attitude towards Jenny is to be found in his account of Nicolas, Restif de la Bretonne. Indeed the story of Nicolas, as Gérard recounts it, again and again throws light on his own ideas and experiences. There were strange resemblances between them, which Gérard himself recognized. One of the most striking analogies is that between Nicholas's love for Mlle Guéant and Gérard's for Jenny. The situations are almost identical. Mlle Guéant was one of the most celebrated young actresses of the Comédie-Française. Like Jenny, she died young, at the age of twenty-four. Nicolas, like Gérard, admired her, 'in the false day of the spot and the footlights', for a whole year before it occurred to him to obtain a closer view of her. Gérard describes him as 'a naïve and simple young man, lover of solitudes and the Latin muses . . . an ideal and Platonic lover, to whom a woman seemed like a fairy, whom he dared not touch for fear of causing his dream to vanish.' The similarity between them is clear. 'Nothing is more dangerous for one of a contemplative nature than a serious love for a stage personality; it is a perpetual delusion, it is the dream of a sick man, it is the illusion of a madman,' Gérard says. . . . 'It was an ideal woman whom he loved, since he had never even dreamed of approaching her.' From the day he waited at the stage door to catch a glimpse of her and followed her home by jumping on to the back of her carriage Nicholas 'felt himself in love with the woman herself and not only with the comedienne'. Meeting her at last, 'he had the strange feeling experienced by all who meet a woman of the theatre face to face for the first time, that of having to make the acquaintance of someone they already know so well'. The difference immediately becomes apparent. The admirer, Nicolas or Gérard, has fallen in love with 'an image I created in my own mind, a fantasy, fugitive as a dream, which I did not even think of realizing, one of those impossibilities I have pursued

<hr>

[1] L. H. Sebillotte, *Le Secret de Gérard de Nerval* (Corti, 1948).

all my life.' Consequently he finds that the real woman corresponds in no way to his exalted vision of her. How could she? She has none of the wit, the intelligence, the charm, the grace, the heart that he has endowed her with in his imagination. Even the face is not the same, and the features no longer resemble so closely those of the other, the ideal, so constantly looked for, so often ephemerally suggested.

There can be little doubt that Gérard's offence was to allow Jenny to become aware of his disillusionment. Her resentment would have been natural, and at the same time Gérard might well have been unconscious of its cause. In the case of Marie Pleyel he was clearly not so deeply involved and, already warned by his previous experience, drew back at the last moment, fearful of a further disappointment. His subsequent resentment towards Marie, as evinced in *La Pandora*, stemmed from self-recrimination for not having proved to himself that he could dominate the situation. His regret for again having 'relinquished the prize for the shadow' now first made him fearful of the possibility of premature physical impotence, the idea of which was to haunt him more and more, as shown by certain obviously subconscious references in *Aurélia*, and would in turn eventually suggest the even greater disaster of a creative impotence which was to prove the final threat to his existence.

Again he fell into a mood of depression and melancholy. One evening, walking along the bank of the Danube, he met his friend Weill. 'What a good way of putting an end to one's life!' he said. Once already, as he had related in a letter to Jenny, he had had a strong impulse to suicide; just now it was no more than a fleeting thought, but the idea remained latent in his mind.

Gérard had been four months in Vienna and it was time to return, but his funds were exhausted. With scarcely enough in his pocket to reach Strasbourg, he wrote desperately for fifty francs for an article to be sent to him there. In order to economize, he decided to travel on foot. The journey took him just over three days, and he reached Strasbourg on 13 March 1840, 'dying of hunger'. When at last he arrived in Paris, it was, he says, 'with as much enthusiasm as I left it last year'.

8

Descent into Hell

Despite the charm and gaiety of Vienna Gérard's mind had been much occupied with the same interests and problems as of old. He had happened to meet there a Prussian consul who was a mesmerist and who had 'produced a great effect among the ladies'. This recalled an old project which had long been neglected, a dramatization of Hoffmann's tale, *The Mesmerist*. He had rewritten the scenario and sent it off to the director of the Opéra Comique, observing that it must have a tough vitality, since he had returned to work on it again and again.

Since about 1830 great interest had been shown throughout France in all forms of occultism, mesmerism, spiritualism, secret societies, freemasonry, the cabbala, and oriental religions. Among Gérard's friends, Dumas, who was a mesmerist, as Gérard relates in a letter, once hypnotized a baker's wife and made her perform surprising contortions of which she retained no memory on awakening; Hugo was a keen spiritualist, and regular séances were held at his house in Jersey during his exile; Balzac, George Sand and Baudelaire were all followers of Swedenborg; and Alexandre Weill was familiar with 'all religions and all philosophies' and had his own peculiar notions about the past, the present and the future.

Gérard interested himself in all these things, and more particularly in the survival of spirits and the possibility of communicating with them. Imbued with the general scepticism of the age, he had never been able to accept entirely the tenets of the Christian religion; the simple faith of the aunt who had first instructed him in them was not for him. Yet he was profoundly conscious of his own need for a religion and moreover, perhaps chiefly because he was continually in search of the mother he had never known, one that would ensure the immortality of the soul. 'The apostle who wanted to touch in order to believe was not cursed for it,' he wrote in *Aurélia,* identifying himself in this respect with Thomas. Once again his dual nature is apparent. Potentially and in his heart he was a fervent believer, but his reason demanded irrefutable proofs before he could acquiesce.

Secretly he had suffered the anguish of this inner conflict all his life, and latterly to an increasing extent. It was the discovery of Goethe's *Faust II* that plunged him into occult regions which promised to resolve his difficulties. A translation and a learned expository essay by Henri Blaze had appeared in 1839. Gérard determined to attempt his own translation, and during his stay in Vienna was principally occupied with this. He confined himself to the part which had originally appeared in 1827, entitled *Helen*, and for the rest contented himself with a detailed analysis embodying translations of the more outstanding scenes.

In this work Gérard found a new concept of immortality to satisfy his hunger. Needless to say, it was not altogether Goethe's. Faust, conducted by Mephistopheles outside the present, beyond time, discovers that the past is not annihilated. In outer regions beyond the material world the elected spirits live on, and Gérard adumbrates a *'spiritual synchronism* which would enable us one day to share the knowledge of him who sees at a glance all the future and all the past.' There is, moreover, the possibility of communication with these spirits, who retain a form perceptible to the eyes of those who are able to disengage themselves, if only for an instant, from terrestrial bonds 'by means of dream, hypnotism, or ascetic contemplation'.

Only the Mothers, procreators of all human beings past and future, have the power to restore the form of Helen to the visible world. Descending to the realm of the Mothers, Faust is granted the privilege of seeing her with Paris. He immediately falls in love with her and, by the strength of his aspiration, succeeds in drawing her out of her sphere of existence into his. 'It was a love born of the intellect, of dream and madness, which succeeded in his heart the wholly naïve and simple love of Margaret.' But it is Margaret who finally intercedes for him and rescues him from the machinations of Mephistopheles. As expressed in his interpretation of Goethe, once again it is the reconciliation of opposites within himself for which Gérard is striving.

Back in Paris, he busied himself with preparing the publication of his translation combined with a reissue of his previous translation of the original *Faust*. The volume was published by Gosselin under the title of *Les Deux Fausts*. This provoked a protest from Charpentier, the publisher of Blaze's translation, who threatened to bring an action against Gosselin for having usurped the title which he claimed was his property, at the same time accusing him of deception in that Gérard's translation contained only three scenes out of the thirty in *Faust II*. It was no more than an attempt to protect his own publication, but Gérard considered it a deliberate attempt to discredit his own work and, although he suffered nothing by it materially, he was considerably perturbed by the affair.

In May Théo Gautier left for a journey in Spain, and Gérard took his friend's place in the columns of *La Presse*. But regular work of this kind soon became irksome to him. Normally, as Théo reports, 'he worked while walking, and, from time to time, he would stop abruptly, searching in his deep pockets for a little stitched paper notebook, and write down a thought, a phrase, a word, a recollection, a sign intelligible only to himself and, closing the notebook, would resume his way faster than ever. It was his manner of composition. More than once we heard him express the desire to walk through life along an endless band winding up behind him as he went, on which he would jot down the ideas that occurred to him, so as to constitute, at the end of the way, a volume of one continuous line.' But this manner of composition was too open to interruptions. He would drop into a café and, quietly seated, scribble away at his task regardless of all the noise and the brilliant lights. He could concentrate so intensely that after he had written a few lines he no longer paid any attention to where he was. According to Champfleury, 'He worked furiously until the arrival of someone he knew forced him to take flight. Then he would go to the Café d'Orsay, install himself at an isolated table and spread out all his working materials. He would scarcely have written two lines when a friend would appear before him and engage him in a long conversation. Gérard would gather up the furnishings of his pockets and leave.'

One night a friend, Hippolyte Lucas, happened to meet him at about one o' clock in pouring rain. His concierge had refused to let him in at that hour, and he was looking for a hotel. Lucas, who lived nearby, offered to put him up. They had a glass of wine or two, and Gérard became talkative. He seemed very excited and talked a great deal about his dramatic projects. When his host saw him to bed, he was still vigorously holding forth in a rather strange manner. At about four or five in the morning Lucas was awakened by a noise; it was Gérard who, finding himself cold, was trying to light the fire. 'If I were of a superstitious nature,' said Lucas, 'you might have frightened me.' Whereupon Gérard began talking of spirits, of the reality of revenants, quoting Hamlet's words, 'there are more things in heaven and earth, Horatio, than are dreamt of in our philosophy'. He went on to explain his theories about the occult sciences in such detail and at such length that his host fell asleep again. In the morning Lucas found Gérard reading a book from his library. But he had become silent now. During lunch he said nothing. Afterwards he thanked his host and took his leave.

To his friends generally Gérard appeared perfectly normal, but this incident and his undue disturbance at Charpentier's objection to the title of his book show that even at this time he was in a state of nervous excitability. He had grown restless again, too, and was anxious to be off on his travels once more. Only his obligation to supply Théo's place during his absence kept him in Paris. But Gautier was delayed on his travels, so that it was not until the middle of October that Gérard was free to leave. This time he planned to go to Brussels. He had learned that *Piquillo* was to be presented there with Jenny in the leading part. He could not hope to be received by her again; such a thought had not even entered his head, for he had resigned himself to his rejection. But he could not entirely forget her and, although the woman was lost to him, the actress, the star, remained to claim his faithful tribute of mute admiration.

He timed his journey accordingly, stopping for a while on the way at Lille and Courtrai. But on arriving in Brussels he was told that most of the actors were ill and that the production of *Piquillo* had been postponed for at least a month. To pass the time he went on to Malines and Antwerp, then to Ghent, Liège, Spa and Namur. He visited buildings and art galleries, but he was also occupied in translating the poems of Heine, whom he had several times visited in Paris. This work occupied much of his time in Belgium. Apart from the fact that he found the air heavy and was suffering from frequent headaches, it was no easy task for him, for he was never fluent in the German language. In November he wrote to Heine, 'I have profited by the leisure that the bad weather has afforded me, to do as much of the translation as possible; but I have still finished only about a third of the work. Nevertheless by working twice as hard when I return, I shall probably be able to complete it in little more than two months. . . . Sometimes I have great difficulty, less in understanding than in rendering, and I have left aside several doubtful meanings until I can consult you. I have even provisionally omitted some poems that I found too difficult; the admirable richness of certain details sometimes makes me uncertain whether to use a German phraseology or to give a French equivalent, but as you have promised to help me, I have left, as I say, only the most important points to refer to you, in order not to waste too much of your time.' None the less, as Heine himself said, 'without understanding German very well, he divined the sense of a poem in German better than those who have made a lifetime's study of the language.' At the same time he was writing his regular articles about his travels and was engaged, too, on an official report on the question of French copyright in Belgium.

News of the forthcoming presentation of *Piquillo* brought him back to Brussels early in December. He had expected to be back in Paris before the end of November, but the delay in the production kept him waiting, with the result that as usual he was running short of money. On the other hand living was comparatively cheap in Belgium. He was well received and entertained everywhere in the capital, his name being already known not only as the author of *Léo Burckart,* a Belgian edition of which had recently appeared, but also as part author of *Piquillo*, which was at last presented on 15 December, with some success.

By a happy chance Marie Pleyel was in Brussels at the time and had already made Jenny's acquaintance. Having retained, as we have seen, her kindly feelings for Gérard, it was natural that she should use her good offices to bring about a reconciliation. One evening at a social gathering Gérard found himself for the last time face to face with Jenny. She approached him with a hesitant and rather doubtful smile as an old acquaintance but nothing more. But Gérard read in her look an indication of forgiveness. 'From that moment', he wrote in *Aurélia,* 'it was as if something sacred was mingled with a love which until then had been purely worldly, endowing it with a quality of eternity.'

Suddenly everything seemed to be changed. It was precisely then that payment of a debt fell due and, since Gérard was scrupulous in such matters, he was forced to return to Paris. He arrived there in a state of extreme excitement on 1 January 1841, intending to spend only a few days settling up his affairs before rejoining his two friends in Brussels.

A few days later, towards midnight, he was walking back along the street in which he was staying when, happening to glance up, he noticed the number of a house lit up by a street-lamp. It was 33. Both he and Jenny were thirty-three years old, and he recalled that Christ had died at the age of thirty-three. On looking down again, he found himself staring into the hollow eyes of a pale-faced woman who seemed to him the very image of Jenny. It may be that news had recently reached him of the death of Sophie, Baronne de Feuchères, some two weeks earlier, and that his mind was preoccupied with the idea of death. However that may be, he was immediately convinced that the incident was a forewarning of the death either of Jenny or of himself at the same time next day, and he was inclined to believe that it was his own death that was foretold.

Accordingly on the following morning he went to visit all his friends. Without saying anything about his premonition of the previous night, in his mind he silently bid them all good-bye. He was in a state of extreme nervous excitement, talking volubly but lucidly, as on the occasion of his night with Hippolyte Lucas. In this exalted mood, it seemed to him that he achieved an astonishing eloquence; he discoursed at length, expounding mystical theories and discussing music, painting, and mathematics. Nothing appeared to be beyond the scope of his comprehension. In the evening, after dinner with two friends, one of them, the painter Paul Chenavard, offered to accompany him home, but Gérard said he was not going home.

'Where are you going, then?'

'To the East!' was the strange reply.

Gérard had fixed his eye upon a certain star,[1] the planet Saturn, that seemed to him at that moment to govern his destiny, and he started walking towards it. It was carnival time, and the strange faces and costumes of the people about him agitated and excited him still further. His friend tried to restrain him but Gérard, in his exalted mood, was quite ungovernable. He walked on, singing a mysterious hymn which he seemed to remember having heard in a previous existence. In a sudden ecstasy of aspiration he threw off his clothes and stood with arms outstretched, awaiting the moment when his soul should leave his body and be drawn up by magnetic attraction to the star.

When the night watch came upon him he resisted violently. At the police station to which he was taken he continued to have ecstatic hallucinations but at the same time was fully aware of all that was going on about him. Lying on a camp-bed, he heard voices discussing another man who had been arrested and when the man himself spoke, the voice seemed to Gérard to sound in his own chest. At once convinced that this man was his double and remembering the German tradition according to which the sight of one's *doppelganger* is a warning that one is about to die, he dared not turn to look at him. Two others, whom Gérard imagined to be his friends, came to fetch the man away. 'But I am the one they have come for,' he cried out indignantly, and he became so violent that he had to be locked in a cell.

Next day he was taken to a private asylum in the Rue Picpus. It was there that his friend Weill visited him. Weill was taken into the room and locked in with him. Gérard explained that he had had an ecstatic fever. Then, after taking Weill's hand and looking at it attentively for a while, 'Take off your shoes and socks,' he

[1] He had always been obsessed with this idea of the star of his destiny; e.g. in *Un Tour dans le Nord* he wrote, 'Forward where chance may lead and let us trust in our star; this is the moment to be guided by it.'

said, 'and I will tell you from whom you are descended.' To humour him Weill did so. 'Now I am going to show you my toes,' said Gérard. 'I myself am descended from Napoleon; I am the son of Joseph, the Emperor's brother, who received my mother at Danzig. You are descended from Isaiah; you have all the signs of it.' The attendant had been watching them all the while through the grille in the door, and when Weill wanted to leave she refused to let him out, declaring that she could not tell which of the two was the madder and that he ought to have been sent to her to be locked up also. Gérard laughed heartily. 'That's just what they do,' he said. 'That's how they got me here.' Weill was forced to wait for another half-hour before the doctor arrived and released him.

Gérard's illness lasted about a month. On 5 March he wrote to his father, 'At last I am allowed to read and write and I believe I have fully recovered the best of health. . . . My illness lasted thirteen days, the rest is a capital convalescence.' From the same letter one learns that it was his father and his friends who defrayed his expenses during that time. Gérard promises to reimburse his father as soon as possible, at the same time gently reproaching him for his unfavourable attitude towards him and begging him to conceal his opinion from others lest they, too, should become prejudiced against him. 'I was surprised', he says, 'during my illness (for I was always fully conscious, even when I could not speak) to hear you impart certain details to people who had no need to know of them.' Dr Labrunie had not relaxed his severity towards his son even at this time of crisis. Gérard felt this keenly, and furthermore he began to imagine that there might be a general conspiracy against him. In a letter to Leclerc, one of his friends at the Ministry of the Interior, he recalled that during his travels letters had frequently gone astray or been opened and read by the police, and that from time to time there had been insurmountable difficulties in obtaining money that was due to him. 'Although there was nothing out of the ordinary in my illness since already for a long time I have been subject to similar nervous attacks, I fancied I could discern in many things that have happened to me as much in Paris as in Vienna and Brussels a certain intrigue or at least some concerted game which I cannot quite make out.' He wanted to know exactly how he stood and who had supplied certain funds. Above all he was anxious to be under no obligation to anyone.

Although Gérard now made light of his illness and considered himself quite cured, his friends were not so sure. They were deeply concerned about him. They blamed themselves for not having detected the signs of his approaching madness. Certainly he had his eccentricities, but how could they have foreseen the sudden fits of violence that would overtake the gentle Gérard, in which he would smash glasses and break chairs. Even his most notable oddity of behaviour had seemed at the time no more than a joke to astound the philistines. On that occasion he had appeared in the Palais-Royal arcades leading a lobster on a ribbon, and, when questioned, had replied, 'Why is it more ridiculous to have a lobster to follow one than to have a dog or a cat, a gazelle, a lion, or any other beast? I like lobsters : they are quiet and serious, they know the secrets of the sea, they don't bark and they don't devour one's substance like dogs, which Goethe found so antipathetic, and moreover he was not mad.'

Alexandre Weill in particular was anxious about him. He wrote to Karr in March, 'I do not know how you have found Gérard. After a four hours' conversation with him I must tell you that he is far from being cured . . . it would take me too long to enumerate all the things he said to me, for ordinarily he tells me more than anyone else; but unhappily they prove that his reason still calls for our care and attention, for it is still deranged.' There is corroboratory evidence of this in certain of Gérard's letters written at that time, notably in one to Pierre Bocage which is almost incomprehensible. In another to Leclerc he signed himself as 'A madman who believes he is sensible and who will be if x'. It may be noted that it is in this letter that he first asks to be addressed as 'Gérard de Nerval, because that is my fancy', and from now on all his books and articles were signed in the same way.

Finally on 16 March he wrote to Jules Janin to tell him of his release : 'The weather is so fine that people cannot meet or embrace indoors. I am going to try to come back. Addio.' The note is signed 'G. Napoleon della torre Brunya e Pallanza', evidence enough to show that he was still subject to illusions of grandeur and noble descent. Only a few weeks before, the rumour had gone about that he was dead, and Janin had written an obituary which had appeared in the *Journal des Débats*. Some of Gérard's friends, fearing that this would upset him, tried to keep it from him. Gérard, however, took it in good part. 'To have the opportunity of reading such a panegyric while still living is honour and glory enough to make one dizzy,' was his ironical comment.

Already he was planning further travels and considering how he might obtain a new commission from the ministry to eke out his income from writing. The first part of his account of Viennese life and customs had lately been published in the *Revue de Paris* and its readers were assured that 'the author, suddenly overcome by a violent illness which his friends, too readily alarmed, considered incurable, will be able within a few weeks to resume his description. . . . The danger is passed, and in a few days M. Gérard de Nerval will be restored to his friends and to his normal occupations.'

Unhappily it was a promise based on false hopes. In less than a week he suffered a relapse, and on 21 March he was taken to Dr Esprit Blanche's clinic in Montmartre. Once again he experienced what he called 'the spilling-over of dream into real life'.[1] He could no longer distinguish between vision and reality. The only difference between waking and sleeping was that when he was awake everything was transfigured in his view: people and things were surrounded by a kind of penumbra which altered their shape, and it was only in dreams that he seemed to perceive things clearly. In this state his words and actions were governed by a strange logic of their own, and he was irritated afterwards to find that they had been attributed to wanderings of the mind.

At times he was haunted by the spectre of his dead mother. Again he met, first in the form of a talking bird and then in person, his great-uncle, who convinced him of the fact of immortality. He had visions of a lost Eden, from which his double tried to drive him away. He dreamed of the history of the primitive human race. And one day, he says:

I found myself in a room which formed part of my ancestor's dwelling. Only it seemed to have grown larger. The old furniture shone with a marvellous polish, the carpets and curtains looked as if they had been renovated, daylight three times as bright as the natural day streamed through the window and the doorway, and the air was fresh with the scent of the first warm mornings of spring. Three women were working in this room, and they represented, without exactly resembling them, relations and friends of my youth. Each seemed to possess the features of several of these. The contours of their faces varied like the flame of a lamp, and at every moment one absorbed something of another; the smile, the voice, the colour of the eyes or of the hair, the figure, the familiar gestures were interchanged as if they lived the same life, and each was thus a composite of all, like those types which artists copy from several models in order to realize a complete beauty.

The eldest of them spoke to me in a clear and melodious voice which I recognized having heard in my childhood, and

---

[1] Later in the *Lettres des Flandres* he was to write 'there are days when one moves through life as through a dream.' The two states were becoming less and less distinguishable.

something she said to me, I do not know what, struck me as being profoundly true. But she drew my attention to myself, and I saw that I was dressed in a little brown coat of antique cut, entirely woven of threads as fine as those of spiders' webs. It was neat and elegant, and there was a pleasant smell about it. I felt very young again and very smart in this garment which was the work of their fairy fingers, and I thanked them, blushing like a little child before handsome grown-up ladies. Then one of them rose and went into the garden.

Everyone knows that in dreams one never sees the sun, although one is aware of a much more vivid brightness. Objects and bodies are luminous. I found myself in a little park where heavy bunches of black and white grapes hung from long trellises; as the lady who was conducting me advanced under this arbour, the curves of her body and her garments were continually variegated by the criss-cross shadows of the trellis. She emerged at last, and we found ourselves in an open space. Traces of ancient paths which had once intersected it at right angles were just discernible. For long years cultivation had been neglected, and straggling plants of clematis, hops, honeysuckle, jasmine, ivy and birthwort festooned the sturdy trees with long loops of trailing strands. Branches bent to the ground, laden with fruit, and among tufts of choking grass bloomed a few garden flowers which had reverted to nature.

At intervals here and there grew thick-set groves of poplars, acacias and pines, in the depths of which one caught glimpses of statues blackened by time. Before me I saw a pile of rocks covered with ivy, from among which spurted a fountain of spring water, the musical plashing of which sounded in a basin of still water half-hidden by the broad leaves of water-lilies.

The lady I was following, stretching her slender waist in a movement that set off the folds of her shot taffeta dress, gracefully encircled with her bare arm a tall hollyhock stem. Then, in a bright ray of light, she began to grow larger, in such a way that little by little the garden took on her form, and the beds and the trees became the rosettes and scallops of her dress; while her face and her arms imprinted their outlines on the purple clouds in the sky. So I lost sight of her as she became transfigured, for she seemed to vanish in her own magnitude. 'Oh! don't go away!' I cried. . . . 'For all nature dies with you!'

With these words I pushed my way painfully through the brambles, as if to catch hold of the exalted spirit that was escaping me, but I stumbled against a piece of broken wall, at the foot of which lay the bust of a woman. On taking it up, I was convinced that it was a bust of *her*. . . . I recognized the beloved features, and, looking about me, I saw that the garden had assumed the appearance of a cemetery. Voices were saying 'The universe is plunged in night!'

'This dream,' he continues, 'so happy in its inception, left me in great perplexity. What did it mean? It was only much later that I learned the answer. Aurélia was dead. At first I heard only that she was ill. Owing to my mental condition at the time I felt only a vague sorrow tinged with hope. I believed that I myself had only a short time to live, and I was assured now of the existence of a world where loving hearts are reunited. Besides, she belonged to me far more in her death than in her life.'

It was, in fact, not until the following June that Jenny died. But by now he had realized that 'it is madness to love a woman who no longer loves you,' and he had, as he says, 'committed to the tomb those loves that were compounded of flesh and ashes.'

At last he began to regain his health, although he had not yet recovered the habit of normal human reasoning. But there were long days of calm when he enjoyed the fresh spring air in the extensive garden and the view over the plain. Using pieces of coal and brick he covered the walls with frescoes which he coloured by pressing out the juices of herbs and flowers that he collected. 'One figure always dominated the others; it was that of Aurélia, depicted with the features of a divinity, just as she had appeared to me in my dream.'

It was not until 21 November, eight months after entering Dr Blanche's clinic, that he emerged again, to all appearances completely cured. In excellent bodily health and with a mind as lucid and alert as ever, he could hardly bring himself to admit that he had been ill. As early as April he had written in a letter, 'Happily today the illness has almost completely subsided; I should say the exaltation, as it seemed, of a much too romantic spirit; for I have the misfortune to believe myself always in my right mind. I am fearful of being in a house full of sensible people and that the mad may be outside.' And in August he had indignantly protested to Jules Janin at the mention of him, in an article published in the *Débats,* as being 'confined' in Dr Blanche's establishment. 'Forgive my writing to you with some bitterness, but you must understand that for seven months I have passed for *mad* thanks to your necrological article of 1 March. . . . I shall never be able to present myself anywhere, never be able to marry, never be able to make myself heard seriously.'

Early in November he wrote to Madame Dumas, 'Yesterday I met Dumas, who is writing to you today. He will tell you that I have recovered what it is generally agreed to call my reason, but don't believe it. I am always and have always been the same and I am only astonished that people found me *changed* for several days last spring. . . . The fact is that I have had a very entertaining dream, and now I regret it; I even have to ask myself if it was not more real than what only now seems to me explicable and natural; but as there are doctors and superintendents here who keep watch lest one should extend the territory of poetry at the expense of the public highway, I was not allowed finally to go out and wander among reasonable people until I was prepared to acknowledge formally that I have been *ill*, which injured my self-esteem and undermined my veracity. "Confess! Confess!" they cried to me, as formerly they did to sorcerers and heretics, and in the end to be done with it I agreed to be classed by the doctors as having suffered from a definite affection called indifferently Theomania or Demonomania in the medical dictionary.'

During his confinement his friends had not been idle on his behalf. Owing to the solicitations of Janin and Hugo he was granted a sum of three hundred francs in October from the funds for the encouragement of science and literature, and a further three hundred in April of the following year.

Little is known of Gérard's activities in the year 1842. It was for him a time of sadness and depression. He could not write, and, feeling that he only evoked pity for his recent illness, he avoided society as much as possible. He visited Jenny's grave in the cemetery of Montmartre, and in the autumn made a brief excursion to the seaside but was soon forced to return to Paris owing to bad weather. The curious thing is that it was this period of disaster, disappointment and frustration that gave birth to a new Gérard. The mere journalist and hack-writer was finished. The true creative genius of the man was about to emerge for a brief, bright season of genuinely true and exquisite self-expression.

9

To the East

The premonition of his own death that he had experienced having been dispelled by the actual death of Jenny, Gérard was faced with the task of re-establishing 'a firm footing in reality'. But it was a new and exotic reality that he chose. Just as in his hallucinatory state he had set off to the East in pursuit of a star, so now the star of his destiny in effect drew him towards the Orient. Although in following it he was in conformity with many of his Romantic contemporaries, among them Lamartine, Hugo, Gautier and Dumas, it was not merely the necessity of finding copy for his books and articles that compelled him. He had long dreamed of such a journey. Now he had more urgent reasons for setting out. Some nine months later he wrote to his father, 'after my too-well-known illness, it was important that my return to health should be publicly established; and nothing should prove it better than an arduous journey in the hot countries; this has not been the least of my motives in undertaking it,' and, on setting out, he said that he was undertaking the journey partly in an effort to escape his depression of the previous winter. If these were superficially plausible reasons, there were far stronger compulsions deep within.

Certain hallucinatory visions or dreams during his illness had temporarily convinced him of the immortality of the soul, but as yet he had found no system which could supply irrefutable evidence. The only solution seemed to him to lie in some form of syncretism and with this in mind he formed the plan of going to study some of the more occult religions at their source. Once, flatly accused of having no religion, he exclaimed with surprise, 'I? No religion? I have seventeen at least!' Clearly, too, the journey was intended to provide both an escape and a renewal. Writing of Lebanon, he says, 'Oh, how happy I was to find I had a plan, a purpose, a resolution, something to dream of, something to attain! This country which has restored all the strength and inspiration of my youth was doubtless bound to do no less for me; I had already truly felt that in setting foot on this maternal soil, in plunging again into the venerated springs of our history and beliefs

I was going to arrest the course of my years, that I should make myself a child again at this cradle of the world, young again at the breast of this eternal youthfulness.'

This, then, was his secret ambition: to defy time, to recapture his youth, to re-enter the lost paradise. It was this quest for his own proper country that had first taken him to Germany and the lone journey was to lead him not only through country after country but through the enchanted regions of reverie and dream, of memory and of poetry.

As this was to be an extended journey Gérard abandoned his usual habit of haphazard departure and took some trouble to prepare for it. He had already read a great deal, for he did not want to visit any place without first having read all that he could find on it in descriptive books and memoirs. He had made arrangements for the publication of an account of his travels with various periodicals and with a Belgian publisher, Hauman, and had thereby obtained advances to cover his initial expenses. He had also obtained some sort of official commission, seemingly of an archaeological nature, which enabled him to travel free on the boats of the state lines, paying only for his meals. Possibly with a view to being better informed for this purpose, he travelled with a companion, Joseph Fonfrède, an orientalist ten years his senior.

The travellers took with them plenty of equipment, including camp-beds, linen and plate. There were dictionaries and grammar and conversation books in Arabic to study on the way. 'We are carrying with us everything we need,' Gérard wrote to his father, 'and more besides, even to blue glasses to guard against the dust.' Their luggage also contained a daguerrotype apparatus for taking views of the places they visited, but the variations of temperature in the course of their journey caused the chemicals to deteriorate and this enterprise proved a failure. Although Gérard found so much luggage both troublesome and costly while travelling, he was bound to admit that most of their paraphernalia had its uses later.

They left Paris on 23 December 1842 and, by way of Lyon and Avignon, reached Marseilles before the end of the month. There they made their final purchases and embarked for Malta on 1 January 1843. So far the weather had been cold and wet, but now a warm sun greeted them from a clear sky as if to beckon them eastwards. The itinerary given by Gérard in his final account of their travels is quite unreliable. The book, which appeared in 1851, was made up from innumerable scattered articles which had somehow to be linked together to form a unified whole. It begins with the account of his sojourn in Vienna in the year 1840. At that time he had had a strong desire to proceed down the Danube and so to Constantinople. Lack of money had prevented him. Now the journey had to be made in imagination, but the route had to be changed in order to link up with the eventual reality. Accordingly Gérard explains that he had delayed so long in Vienna that he had missed the last boat for Belgrade and that ice now rendered the river unnavigable. The imaginary journey takes him by train and road to Trieste; thence down the Adriatic, conveniently in such terrible weather that it was 'impossible to see anything more than the misty shores of Illyria on our left and the numerous islands of the Dalmatian archipelago'.

The account is not all evasion, for next comes a long and detailed description of Cerigo, the ancient Cytherea, which incidentally provides the opportunity for a long digression on the loves of Francisco Colonna and Lucrezia Polia, who in dream pledged themselves to each other there for eternity. Even in his description of places he had not seen, Gérard was never at a loss. He always had literary sources to fall back on, besides paintings and engravings. Throughout the book, for example, there are considerable borrowings from such writers as William Lane.

In order to trace the true stages of his journey, we must turn again to his letters. From these we learn that the weather grew worse after they left Marseilles and the passage to Malta took eight days instead of the usual four or five. When they passed Naples, Vesuvius was crowned with snow, as also, a little later, were Stromboli and Etna. They reached Valetta on 8 January and early next day boarded the *Minos* which was to take them through the Greek archipelago to Syra before going on to Egypt.

No call was made at Cerigo, but soon after dawn on 10 January they passed close to its desolate shores where Gérard was able to distinguish, silhouetted against the skyline, a gibbet with three arms, from one of which was suspended the body of a hanged man. It was a depressing sight for one who had imagined 'Watteau's shepherds and shepherdesses landing on the flower-covered shores from boats decorated with garlands', and it seemed to him a sad symbol of the English domination of the island of the celestial Venus. The image he bore away was subsequently to be the source of Baudelaire's famous description in his poem 'A Journey to Cytherea'.

Twenty-four hours at Syra sufficed to furnish Gérard with enough material for three chapters of his book, before the *Minos* sailed again for Alexandria, where she arrived on 16 January. After a short stop in Alexandria, a five-day journey by boat up the Nile brought the travellers to Cairo, where they intended to stay for some time.

Here Gérard found plenty to occupy him. He was not interested in the ordinary 'sights'. He had no wish to be taken for a tourist. His opinion of tourists in general, particularly the English, is obvious from the quietly satirical remarks that crop up here and there in his letters. What interested him were the ordinary sights and incidents of the street. He was as happy wandering about the streets of Cairo as he had been in Paris. The costumes and customs of the people absorbed him. His quick eye caught glimpses of their daily life that might have been overlooked by a more sophisticated traveller. Nothing was too mean for his observation. The result is that this part of his chronicle, although it was worked over again and again during composition, has a convincing air of spontaneity. It is a very individual account, presented with liveliness and humour which retains its power to delight and amuse.

As usual much of Gérard's time was occupied in reading. There were libraries and learned societies to assist him in his research, and he was delighted to find at the Egyptian Society a collection of 'nearly all the books, ancient and modern, which have been published on the country'.

Before they set foot in Alexandria they had been accosted by a dragoman known as Abdullah, who had drawn alongside the *Minos* in a boat and boarded her. This man helped them to find a small house to rent at a moderate cost, and enabled them to furnish it simply but comfortably. It was Gérard's custom, wherever he travelled, to conform as far as possible to the habits of the people among whom he found himself. Now he adopted the costume of a Mohammedan and had his hair and beard cut in the Levantine style. 'I lost my European hair,' he says. 'The barber ran his razor over it with great dexterity, and, at my express demand, left me a single lock on the top of my head like that worn by the Chinese and the Muslims. Opinion is divided as to the reason for this custom : some claim that it is to offer a hand-hold to the angel of death; others discern a more material motive. The Turk always provides for the possibility of being decapitated, and, as it is the custom on such occasions to show the head to the public, he does not want it to be held up by the nose or the lips, which would be most ignominious. The Turkish barbers spite the Christians by shaving them completely bare; as for me, I was superstitious enough not to reject any superstition.'

The *Voyage en Orient* abounds in such ironic treatment of his experiences. It matters little that the sights and incidents recorded are sometimes drawn from other sources. Throughout the book, the material is thoroughly assimilated and becomes his own by virtue of the unity of style and expression he imposes on it.

Gérard, who in the book pretends to be travelling alone, makes much of the story of Zeynab. According to the published version of the episode, shortly after setting up house, he was visited by the local sheik who informed him that it was not customary for a man to live alone and that if he wished to remain in the district he must choose a woman to live with him, in order not to arouse the suspicions of his neighbours. After considering the pros and cons of various possible marriages with women of different sects, he finally accepts Abdullah's suggestion that he should purchase a slave. There follows the tale of Zeynab, the beautiful Javanese slave whom he takes to live with him, partly hoping to economize by saving the expense of a cook, but when he proposes that she should take her turn at preparing a meal, she indignantly protests that she is a lady now and not a servant. This account provides a narrative thread on which to string his descriptions of actual events, his observations and his comments.

The true facts upon which the story is based appear in the correspondence. In a letter to his father he writes, 'they wanted me to marry a twelve-year-old Syrian girl; but I found her a little too young,' and more pertinently in a letter to Théo, speaking of his fellow-traveller, whom he describes as 'quite agreeable. . . . 'He has bought an Indian slave. . . . This woman costs a lot of money and we scarcely know what to do with her. There are as many other women available as one could wish for. One can get married in the Coptic or in the Greek manner, and it is much cheaper than buying a woman, as my companion has been stupid enough to do. They are trained in the ways of the harem, and they have to be waited on; it is tiresome.' It would seem probable that the young girl referred to in the letter to his father was a daughter of M. Linant de Bellefonds or Linant Bey, engineer, archaeologist and explorer, who was then Director General of roads and bridges for the Viceroy of Egypt and who later, in 1845, supervized the preliminary work on the Suez Canal. It was at the house of the French consul, Gauttier d'Arc, with whom he had become very friendly, that Gérard first met him, and the girl would have been one of the 'four or five young persons, white or bronzed, in very brilliant dresses' whom Gérard at first took to be members of M. Linant's seraglio, but who turned out to be his marriageable daughters.

The two companions remained in Cairo for three months. They had intended to leave earlier, but on receiving news that the plague had broken out in Beirut they decided to stay on. Their plan was to take a boat from Damietta to Jaffa and then to proceed to Beirut by way of St John d'Acre. Before they left they made an excursion to the pyramids. In recounting their visit Gérard seizes the opportunity to describe certain ancient ceremonies of initiation. At once it becomes clear where his real interest lies. Signs of this preoccupation might already have been detected beneath the gay and colourful surface of the first part of his book, as in the description of the Dervishes where some tentative suggestions of a possible syncretism are made. But now the whole journey begins to emerge as a form of initiation of the traveller into ancient mysteries. Fantasy and fact are so skilfully interwoven that the reader only gradually realizes that Gérard is engaged in a journey on two separate levels. From now on his spiritual journey in search of the art of deciphering the symbolism of human existence increasingly obtrudes upon the lively narrative.

In Syria it was the religion of the Druses that particularly captured his imagination. 'The Druses', he says, 'have been compared with the Pythagoreans, the Essenes, and the Gnostics, and it seems that the Templars, the Rosicrucians and the modern Freemasons borrowed many of their ideas from them.' Here was a religion that promised to satisfy his esoteric inclinations. He sees in 'the belief of the Druses . . . nothing but a syncretism of all preceding religions and philosophies.' He finds that they believe in metempsychosis and that although men have no consciousness of their transmigrations, 'the faithful can, in raising themselves by the nine stages of initiation, gradually arrive at a knowledge of all things and of themselves.' Such a Faustian aspiration could not fail to appeal to Gérard. He even dreamed of adopting their faith and marrying a Druse.

The two stories which he incorporated in the account of his travels, pretending to have had one from a sheik and the other from a story-teller in Istanbul, are fables of man in search of his true spiritual self. Between them they embody the whole of the Nervalian mythology. The first is the legend of Hakem, founder of the Druse religion. In Gérard's version the story resumes something of his own attitudes and experiences. Like Gérard, Hakem is in love with the unattainable, in this case his sister Setalmulc whom nevertheless, having become aware of his own divinity, he is determined to marry. This decision is in part the cause of his downfall, for by the machinations of his jealous vizier Argevan, disguised one evening as an ordinary citizen, he is arrested and locked up in a mad-house for having pretensions to be not only the caliph but also God. Meanwhile Setalmulc and Yousouf, his double, have fallen in love. Yousouf declares that 'this divine face was already known to me. Yet when had I seen it before? In what world had we met? What previous existence had brought us together? I cannot tell.' This woman completely realizes his ideal, and he has the conviction that he has loved her 'for all eternity'. Hakem escapes and returns to his palace to find it lit as for a fête. Greatly disturbed by the fact that nobody recognizes him or pays any attention to him, he passes like an invisible phantom through the crowd of slaves and pages, and at last comes upon his sister and his double seated side by side as bride and bridegroom. Realizing the significance of this confrontation with his double, he is powerless to intervene. It is the same obsessional theme that is found again in *Aurélia*. That same night Hakem is attacked by three men. One of them is his double, Yousouf, who, suddenly recognizing him, turns to his defence. Both Hakem and Yousouf are killed, but their bodies – or perhaps the body – mysteriously disappear, never to be found.

The other tale, the legend of Adoniram, is even more significant in relation to Gérard's life. It is also the story of the Queen of Sheba, the beautiful Balkis, Queen of the South, developed from the scenario of the opera that in 1834 Gérard had intended for Jenny Colon. But now it has become a mystical story in which Gérard expresses a sense of his own destiny through that of Adoniram, the mysterious master craftsman who has supervized the building of Solomon's Temple. At the time when Balkis comes to visit Solomon, Adoniram is engaged in preparing his greatest work, the Sea of Brass. The king grows jealous of Adoniram when, at Queen Balkis's request, he summons all his workmen before her by means of a magic sign and is rewarded with a symbolic gift, a sun made of precious stones set in a golden triangle on a necklace of pearls, which she takes from her own neck and places round his. Solomon is alarmed at Adoniram's magic power over men, fearing that 'a movement of his brows would make him king of Israel'. At last everything is ready for the casting of the Sea of Brass. The people gather to watch the dangerous operation. Suddenly the treachery of some of the workmen brings about disaster. The cast explodes in a rain of fire, killing many and scattering the rest. Adoniram is left alone. Then out of the flames the figure of Tubal Cain appears and conducts him into the subterranean world, 'the domain of your fathers. Here the race of Cain reigns alone. Beneath these granite fortresses, within the inaccessible caverns, we have been able to find liberty. It is here that the tyranny of Adonai expires, here that one can feed on the fruit of the Tree of Knowledge without perishing,' and he explains that it is the sanctuary of fire which provides warmth for the earth and its inhabitants; all would perish from the cold were

1   Nerval aged twenty-three. Bronze medallion by Jehan Duseigneur
Photo Bulloz

3 Marie Pleyel
Bibliothèque Nationale

2 Jenny Colon
Bibliothèque Nationale

it not for the work of the race of Cain. Adoniram returns to repair his work. Aware now of his own true origin, by his mastery of her wonderful hoopoe, which will obey none but the noblest of her line, he reveals to Balkis their common ancestry, recognizing in her his sister and predestined spouse. But it is not their destiny to be united on earth; treachery and jealousy intervene, and he is stabbed to death in the temple.

These myths are the source of many of the dreams and visions in *Aurélia.* Both Balkis and Aurélia are images of the ideal woman, at once queen, goddess and star; sister, mother and bride; now to be identified with Isis, now with the Virgin Mary. Gérard himself 'beneath the blood-stained pallor of Abel' has 'sometimes borne the implacable mark of Cain'. Like Adoniram he believes himself to be one of the 'children of the fire', inhabitants of the kingdom of Enoch or Hermes who, in revolt against the tyranny of Adonai or Jehovah who has condemned men and planets to ultimate extinction, tend in secret the central fire of life. Both, in fact, are men in revolt against an unjust destiny.

Gérard had been forced to leave the Lebanon at the beginning of July, having contracted a fever, and he may well have actually experienced fantastic visions like these while he was in a state of mental excitement similar to that of his earlier illness. They were symptomatic of his later mental disorder.

After visiting Cyprus, Rhodes and Smyrna, he arrived in Constantinople towards the end of July. Already he was experiencing some depression and disillusion. Even of his stay in Cairo he had written, 'some days I grow sad; for I would not say that eternal summer always makes life happy. The black sun of melancholy, which casts its dark rays over the brow of Albrecht Dürer's dreaming angel, also sometimes rises over the brightly lit plains of the Nile, as over the banks of the Rhine, in a cold German landscape.' And again 'I am leaving regretfully this old city of Cairo, where I have found again the last traces of Arab genius, and which has not betrayed the ideas I had formed from the stories and traditions of the Orient. I had seen it so many times in my childhood's dreams that it seemed to me I had stayed there I don't know when; I reconstructed my former Cairo in the midst of deserted quarters or crumbling mosques! It seemed to me that I set my feet in my own footprints of old; as I walked I said to myself: Going round this wall, passing this door, I shall see such and such a thing . . . and there it was, ruined but real. Let us think no more of it. That Cairo lies beneath ashes and dust; the spirit of modern progress has triumphed over it like death.' Yet he still had the passion of the traveller: 'In Africa, one dreams of India, as

D

in Europe one dreams of Africa; the ideal always beams beyond our actual horizon.'

Now, however, he was growing tired. From Constantinople he wrote to his father, 'Here I am at last in Europe; here I find once more my beloved French papers, but what annoyances, what heat, what quarantines in order to arrive in this almost civilized region! I am rather tired of the mountains, of the dust, and of the half-wild people of Carmel and Lebanon. It is very lovely at a distance, and very tiresome at close quarters.' And to Théo he wrote, 'As for me, I have lost kingdom by kingdom, and province by province, the more beautiful half of the universe, and soon I shall no longer know where to give refuge to my dreams; but it is Egypt that I regret most having chased from my imagination, to place it sadly in my memories! . . . You still believe in the ibis, in the purple lotus, in the yellow Nile; you believe in the emerald-green palm-tree, in the Barbary fig, in the camel perhaps. . . . Alas! the ibis is an unsociable bird, the lotus a common onion; the Nile is a reddish river with slate-coloured reflections, the palm-tree looks like a lank feather-broom, the Barbary fig is nothing but a cactus, the camel exists only as a dromedary, the dancers are males, and as for the real women, it would seem that one is happy not to see them.'

After leaving Egypt he had been delighted to see clouds again: 'O blessed clouds! clouds of my own country! I had forgotten your delights!' His thoughts were turning to France, and he was looking forward to seeing his friends again. Meanwhile by a happy chance he found one of them in Constantinople. It was Camille Rogier, his old friend and companion of the Rue du Doyenné, who had left France in 1837 and, after spending three years in Florence and Rome, had moved on to Athens and then to Constantinople, where he had finally settled and where his paintings were in great demand.

Early in September Gérard's travelling-companion had to return to France to attend a lawsuit. Gérard himself stayed on, for he was anxious to witness the festivals of Ramadan. Although he was able to place some articles with the Constantinople papers he was not well paid for them, and once again his funds were running low. However Rogier found him cheap lodgings in the district between the Golden Horn and the sea at the Ghildiz Khan or Star Hotel, a name whose symbolic connotations evidently appealed to his imagination. It was a large rambling building filled with Persians and Armenians. To be in keeping with them he adapted his Cairo outfit merely by adding an Astrakhan hat to it. His room was austerely bare, furnished only with a mat, a bamboo table and his camp-bed. By foregoing wine he found he could live cheaply and comfortably enough.

He was now in good health and spirits. As he wrote to his father, he was not easily discouraged; he had determination and relied on that to carry him through temporary difficulties. It was only the fear of sickness that troubled him, for 'a man of letters, like an artist, has only himself to rely on and he must therefore have complete control of all his faculties. Once ill or discouraged, all is lost.'

The prospect of returning to France cheered him. He had been well received everywhere, but what he missed most was music and lighted rooms. For too long he had been out of touch with the life of Paris, and it pleased him to learn that Théo had dedicated a new ballet, *Giselle,* to Gérard who had originally inspired it. His anxiety to be back infected Rogier, and when Gérard left at the beginning of November Rogier went with him. From Malta, which they reached on 16 November, he wrote to his friend Jules Janin, 'although everywhere one meets honest and lovable people, they are never as valuable as those whom one has known and loved for a long time, and with whom one was young. . . . I have had enough of running after poetry; I believe it is at one's door and perhaps in one's bed. I am still a man running, but I am going to try to stop and wait.'

He was conscious of growing older. He had always suffered a little from short-sightedness, but now it was more pronounced. His hair was thinning, and he was growing stouter. His beard was a little less carefully trimmed. There was a certain stiffness of the joints, and again at Malta he had a slight attack of fever.

Anxious as he was to return, he could not resist a second visit to Naples. Pompeii in particular attracted him and this time, despite his dislike of railways, he was pleased to find that it was now possible to make the excursion from Naples by train as far as Torre Anunciata, and much more cheaply than on his previous visit. Again his goal was the ruined temple of Isis. After his esoteric researches in the near East, what was he in search of? 'Child of a sceptical rather than an incredulous generation, wavering between two contrary influences, that of the Revolution, which denied everything, and that of the social reaction, which pretends to bring together all Christian beliefs, would I be led to believe everything, as our fathers the philosophers had been led to deny everything?' It was the vision of Isis herself that he sought, 'the fundamental identity of this queen of heaven, of divers attributes and changing countenance', as she had appeared to Lucius Apuleius, describing herself as 'the mother of nature, mistress of the elements, prime source of the ages, greatest of divinities, queen of shades; I who mingle in myself both gods and goddesses; I whose unique and all-powerful divinity the universe has adored under a thousand forms. So in Phrygia I am called Cybele; at Athens, Minerva; in Cyprus, Paphian Venus; in Crete, Diana Dictymine; in Sicily, Stygian Proserpine; at Eleusis, the antique Ceres; elsewhere, Juno, Bellone, Hecate or Nemesis, whilst the Egyptians, who preceded all other peoples in the sciences, render me homage under my true name of the goddess Isis.'

In *Octavie* Gérard relates the story of an assignation with an English girl, the 'syren of the grottoes', at this same temple, where she enacted the part of Isis and he that of Osiris. This was probably pure fantasy, but it is possible that on this second visit he did meet again the young woman he calls Octavie, now tied to a paralytic husband.

After ten days in Naples, he went on by boat to Leghorn, Genoa and Marseilles where he arrived on 5 December and was met by Méry and other friends, including Camille Rogier whom he had left at Malta. Christmas was spent with Rogier's family at Nîmes, and he finally reached Paris after his twelve months' travel early in the new year, 1844.

It had been a year of the greatest significance for him. At the close of his account of it in the *Voyage en Orient* he wrote, 'Must I defend myself in your view for my successive admiration for the different religions of the countries I have visited? Yes, I have felt myself to be a pagan in Greece, a Mohammedan in Egypt, a pantheist among the Druses, and at sea a devotee of the star-gods of Chaldea; but in Constantinople I comprehended the grandeur of that universal tolerance exercised today by the Turks.' He had found that the fundamental truths were common to all religions, and he illustrates his point with a parable. Four travelling companions, a Turk, an Arab, a Persian and a Greek are to take a meal together. They club together and subscribe their few coins. But what are they to buy? '*Uzum*, said the Turk – *Ineb*, said the Arab – *Inghir*, said the Persian – *Stafilion*, said the Greek. Each of them wanted to impose his own preference on the others. They had nearly come to blows when a dervish who knew all four languages intervened. He called to a raisin-seller, and it turned out that raisins was what each of them was demanding.'

10

Life in Paris

Back in Paris Gérard was quickly involved in the old routine. The restlessness that drove him from country to country and prevented him, when at home, from pinning himself down to fixed hours of work, still forced him into a ceaseless activity. As usual after his travels his meagre resources were exhausted. He planned an illustrated edition of his account of his journey to Egypt, and considered that he had enough material to occupy him for at least two years. It was his ambition to publish it in book form without first having recourse to the journals, for he thought this would give his work a greater status in the eyes of the public. But his immediate needs had to be met. Besides taking up dramatic criticism again, he contributed articles and stories to a number of periodicals. Thus much of his material had already been utilized when finally, in 1851, the *Voyage en Orient* was published. The projected volume of the journey in Egypt never appeared separately.

After a year's absence his old friendships were eagerly renewed. He made new friends, among them Baudelaire, and he resumed his wanderings by night in Montmartre, in the markets and in some of the more squalid quarters. The sights and sounds, the clear skies of the near East faded like a dream. Only the abundant notes he had brought back upon which he was working intermittently kept those scenes alive in his imagination.

In spite of the keen delight he had expressed at returning, it was not long before he was again overcome by the urge to travel, and in September 1844 he set off for Belgium and Holland in company with Houssaye. Writing to his father on the 23rd from Amsterdam, he says, 'I have seen Rotterdam, which is a very beautiful city, Antwerp, the Hague and Haarlem. It is all magnificent and as singular as I expected. I am going to stay here three days and shall be in Paris two or three days later.' It was a brief tour, but, although he was all the while sending back articles to the Paris papers, it released him temporarily from the strain of his regular contributions and distracted him for a while from the anxieties of his hand-to-mouth existence.

At Haarlem he had been particularly interested in the story of Laurent Coster, a print-seller of that city who, according to a Dutch legend, had been the inventor of printing in the fourteenth century. The plan of a dramatic production on the subject was beginning to germinate. But suddenly his thoughts took a new and unexpected turn. He was inspired with the notion of inventing his own printing machine. Having studied for a time the technicalities of typography, he set to work on an invention which he fondly hoped would speedily make his fortune.

'Unhappily,' he wrote later in the play that finally emerged, 'the heads of all these inventors, all these men of genius are wholly occupied with a mad mistress, a woman who does not exist and who is named imagination; they pursue her all their life, they sacrifice everything to this dream, they build for her beautiful castles in Spain, and forget their home and their work.' Even though Gérard himself was subject to this same misfortune, the dream that he pursued was of a different order. But he had patience and determination, and on 5 January 1845 he was granted a patent for 'a machine for printing by means of movable rows of letters, which he calls a stereograph'. No model was ever made, but it appears to have been a sort of forerunner of the Linotype. It was a small machine, which could be placed upon a table. A series of round metal discs bearing the letter types in a band round their circumferences were to be revolved each independently about a central axis. When the line of type was thus composed, it was to be stamped down on to the printing surface on the bed of the machine. Although Gérard renewed his patent for the following year also, no sponsor for the machine appeared, and the idea was soon forgotten.

Meanwhile he had resumed his work in Paris and had again taken over his friend Théo's column in *La Presse* for three months while he was travelling in Algeria. But in August 1845 he managed to escape for eight days to London. In his *Nuits d'Octobre* he mentions the fact that he had visited England three times, and it is almost certain that he first crossed the Channel for a brief spell during his journey with Théo in 1836, the evidence for this being an article on English customs and a poem on the passage from Ramsgate to Antwerp, which begins : 'To the English coast/ I have said goodbye./ Its white cliffs are lost/ at the edge of the sky.' Of this second visit in 1845 he wrote, in *Un Tour dans le Nord,* 'I wholeheartedly share the opinion of Nestor R[oqueplan], who said that a land that cannot be approached from any direction without undergoing excruciating colics isn't a country at all. It [i.e. England] is so little of a country, in fact, that its inhabitants, as far as they

can, make themselves citizens of the whole world. I have been told
of an English couple who, wanting to see the Continent, suffered
so much during a rough crossing that they never wanted to risk
another sea voyage – they came to live near Boulogne and pass
their lives there, gazing towards the coast of their motherland,
where, moreover, they wish one day to be buried. They hope that
when one is dead one does not suffer from sea-sickness any more.
A weighty question.'

Nevertheless he seems to have returned on a third visit in 1849.
He was attracted to England chiefly by its literature, in particular
Shakespeare, Sterne, Swift, Scott and Dickens, but all his travels
were undertaken partly in the constant search for copy; and the
journey of 1845 supplied him with at least the brief vignette which
forms Section V of his *Nuits d'Octobre*, written in the form of a
conversation with a friend :

'Have you been to London?'
  'Three times.'
  'Well, then, you are acquainted with the splendour of its
nights, from which too often the sun of Italy is missing? When
one emerges from Majesty Theatre [*sic*], or Drury Lane, or
Covent Garden, or even from the charming intimacy of the
Strand, under the direction of Mme Céleste, one's spirit stirred
by the music, noisy or delightfully soothing (oh the Italians!)
. . . by the jokes of some clown or other, or by the boxing bouts
that one watches from a box . . . one's spirit, I say, feels the
need – in this happy city where there are no door-porters, where
it has never been thought of inventing them – to relax from the
tension. Then the crowd rushes into the *beef-houses*, the *oyster-
houses,* the societies, the clubs and the bars!'
  'You need not tell me! London nights are delightful; they are
a series of paradises or a series of hells, according to one's means.
The *gin-palaces* resplendent with gas-light, mirrors and gilding,
where one gets tipsy between an Englishman who is one's equal
and a rag-picker . . . The thin little girls who offer to sell you
flowers. The ladies who, walking home from Vauxhall and the
theatre galleries, jostle you in the English way, astonish you by
their comradely indifference. Velvets, ermines, diamonds, as at the
Queen's theatre! . . . So that one wonders whether it isn't the
great ladies who are . . .'
'Shh!'

For the next few years there was to be no more travelling. His
work kept him in Paris, and during the year 1846 the only

excursions he permitted himself were to the country of his childhood. He had been led back to it first perhaps by his memory of
its songs and legends which he had known so well in his early
years. He had first published a study of these in the *Sylphide* in
1842. He was one of the first to appreciate the simplicity of the
popular ballads, to collect them and to reproduce them in their
original form without trying to improve them. He complains that
songs in dialect from Brittany or Aquitaine had been preserved but
none of the songs in the true French tongue from Valois, because
'Verses composed without care for rhyme or prosody or syntax'
were generally ignored, and adds that 'the language of the shep-
herd, the sailor, the passing carter, is truly ours, apart from some
elisions, dubious turns of speech, risqué words, odd terminations and
liaisons, but it bears the stamp of ignorance which revolts educated
people more than dialect does. None the less this language has its
rules, or at least its regular practices.' Music, he points out, 'lends
itself admirably to such ingenuous boldness, and discovers in the
assonances, employed sparingly enough, all the resources which
poetry should provide.'

During the succeeding years right up to the time of his death
he returned again and again to the Valois country, and these
ramblings recalled to him the scenes and impressions on which were
built *Angélique, Sylvie* and the *Promenades et Souvenirs.* 'The
memories of childhood are revived', he wrote, 'when one reaches
middle age. It is like a manuscript palimpsest the lines of which
are made to reappear by chemical processes.'

As he wandered about that quiet countryside, the memories
flowed back. There he rediscovered the archery ranges with the
platforms for the distribution of prizes, and the dancing grounds
with benches for the old people who had gathered round to
enjoy the spectacle of the younger folks' enjoyment. Wandering
about the ruins of Châalis Abbey, he ascended the tower. 'From
there could be seen the whole of the valley, intersected by ponds
and rivers, and with the bare stretches known as the Desert of
Ermenonville, of grey sandstone interspersed with spare pines and
heather. Reddish-coloured quarries stood out here and there against
the leafless woods and enlivened the greenish tint of the plains and
forests, where the white birches, their trunks bound with ivy and
still bearing the last leaves of autumn, were still clearly defined
against the red-tinted masses of the woods framed by the blue
haze of the horizon.'

Again he visited Ermenonville, that region, 'where the names of
Erman or Armen are common in the neighbourhood.' Ermenonville,
he declares, is 'called in the district Arme-Nonville or Nonval',

clearly associating the name with Nerval. The place was also essentially associated for him with Rousseau, and he visited his grave. 'Rousseau's tomb remains as it was, with its simple antique form, and the poplars, leafless now, still picturesquely adorn the monument, which is reflected in the still water of the lake.' It pleased him to find still preserved 'certain customs which one does not find any more elsewhere. They still play in the streets there, they talk, they sing in the evening on the doorsteps.' He loved, no less than Rousseau, the distant sound of the church bells and he delighted in the misty autumn landscapes. 'Tired of the vain wranglings and the sterile bustle of Paris, I find rest in contemplating again these fields which are so green and fruitful; I regain my strength on this maternal soil.' It was the birth of an irresistible nostalgia that was to call him back again and again in succeeding years.

Meanwhile, back in Paris, under the compelling necessity to earn sufficient money for his modest needs, he was condemned to the daily drudgery of journalism and since by nature he was not a prolific writer he was frequently forced to make use of his material more than once, sometimes reworking it entirely. Now, however, remembering perhaps the initial success of *Piquillo,* he turned again to the theatre. In collaboration with Alboize he began work on *Les Montenegrins,* based on an episode of the Balkan revolution, for which Limnander, whom he had met in Belgium, was to compose the music. The work was completed and submitted to the board of censors on 19 February 1848. Three days later the revolution broke out and on 24 February, Louis Philippe abdicated. On the 29th, Gérard, together with Esquiros, Marc Fournier, Alexandre Weill, and Considérant, founded the *Club des Augustins.* But he took no real interest in politics. It was literature alone that claimed him. Once again reduced to a spare economy, he found a cheap lodging in the Rue St Thomas du Louvre, very near the old Rue du Doyenné. But how his circumstances were changed now! The wretched, tumbledown building was already designed for demolition, and the quarter had an unsavoury reputation. He scarcely dared to confess to his friends where he was living, and no one visited him there.

For some years he had been translating Heine's poems, but had awaited the opportunity to elucidate certain passages by consulting Heine before completing the work, and during the following month the two poets met regularly for this purpose. 'I cannot think, without deep emotion,' Heine wrote in 1853 in his preface to the translation, 'of those evenings in the month of March, 1848, when the good and gentle Gérard came to see me every day in my retreat near the Santé gate, to work tranquilly with me on the translation of my quiet German musings,' and he went on to say:

Unhappily, my friend Gérard, even on his lucid days, was liable to continual distractions, and I discovered, but too late to remedy the omission, that he had mislaid seven passages in the series which comprises the 'North Sea'. I have left these lacunae in my poem so as not to interfere with the unity of the whole, the harmonious colour and rhythm of which might have been spoilt by the interpolation of my own rude attempts. Gérard's diction flowed with a smooth purity which was inimitable and which can only be compared with the sweetness of his spirit. He was in truth more of a spirit than a man, the spirit of an angel, however trite the phrase may seem. His spirit was essentially sympathetic. And he was a great artist; the perfumes of his thought were always enclosed in marvellously chased containers. Moreover he had nothing of the artist's egoism: he was all childlike candour; he was extremely sensitive; he was kind, he loved everybody; he was never jealous of anyone; he never scratched anyone.

The latter part of this encomium was echoed by Jules Janin, who wrote, 'He was loved by everybody; he was never under obligation to anyone, he never flattered anyone, he never let anyone down; so that everyone loved and honoured him.'

The two poets had much in common. They worked together happily and in perfect harmony, growing to be close friends. For all his sympathetic understanding, the translations had proved no easy task for Gérard, but now, with Heine's help, the last difficulties were resolved, and the work was finally published by the *Revue des Deux Mondes* in July and September.

The production of *Les Montenegrins* having been put off because of the revolution, Gérard was forced to seek other means of revenue. On 1 March 1849 his serial novel, *Le Marquis de Fayolle,* began to appear in *Le Temps.* Gérard was no novelist and the story, of the uprising of the Chouans in Brittany in the eighteenth century, is interesting only as it embodies many of the typical Nervalian themes and obsessions. Like Gérard, the Marquis 'had read the learned musings of the Abbé de Villars, of Dom Pernety, and of the Marquis of Argens,' and moreover he had even 'taken part in the famous gatherings at Ermenonville, presided over by the Count Saint Germain.' His conversation was stamped with Swedenborgian mysticism. In the person of the hero, Georges, Gérard deplores the loss of his own mother and expresses the subconscious antagonism to his father that soured their private relationship. Again the theme of the childish mock-marriage is introduced. Georges reminds Gabrielle how, when they were children, 'that good woman led us into her room and showed us her wedding clothes and those of her husband. . . . Do you remember? There was nothing but velvet and taffeta. So that we had the idea of putting them on; we found we were big enough to look like a young married couple.' And, as later in *Sylvie*, the young lovers assume the characters of the Julie and Saint Preux of the *Nouvelle Héloïse*.

Gérard kept up his regular instalments with difficulty. On 27 March they were interrupted. They were continued on 26 April, but on 28 May readers were informed that '*Le Temps* will resume publication of the third part of M. Gérard de Nerval's fine novel on 6 June.' Political events had again interfered to distract readers, but before this Gérard had suffered a relapse brought about by the continual strain of his work combined with a new disappointment. *Les Montenegrins* had been produced at last on 31 March at the Opéra Comique and had been well received by the public, but the cholera epidemic, which had broken out on 3 March and which was to claim sixteen hundred victims before the end of the summer, very soon emptied the theatres and forced them to close. It was a heavy blow to Gérard, who had expected much from the piece.

In April he was taken into the care of a friend, Dr Amedée Aussandon. This second attack was far less severe than the first of 1841, eight years before, and at first there was no need for strict confinement. He was able to visit his friends and dine with them, but there were similar, if less pronounced, symptoms of disturbance, and in May he was under the care of Dr Ley in his private hospital. However, the illness was of short duration, and by the end of the month he was able to visit London again for several weeks.

He returned to Paris in time to witness the uprising of 13 June, among the leaders of which were some of his friends, notably Considérant. The cholera epidemic was subsiding, but people were still terrified of it. As Gérard wrote in a letter to Théo, who was in London, 'People take to their beds for the slightest indisposition which they would have taken no notice of ordinarily.' Ernesta Grisi, Théo's mistress, was, he told him, in perfect health. 'We went to dinner at Madame Heine's, who was taken ill during the meal, but who is better. La Presidente[1] also had an attack the day before yesterday. The Turgue too, but it is all trifling and the result of

---

[1] Aglae Josephine Savatier (1822–1889), known as Aglae Apollonie Sabatier, 'la Presidente' celebrated by Baudelaire.

indiscretions, artichokes in the case of the Heine household, lobster in that of La Presidente, and I don't know what in Turgue's.'

The Turgue referred to was Julien Turgan, an intern at the Charité hospital, who was passionately interested in aerial locomotion. On one occasion he travelled for a whole night in a balloon with four others. He wrote a book on balloons, to which Gérard contributed an introduction. As early as 1839 Gérard in his *Notes de Voyage* had shown some interest in 'the appearance at the Champ-de-Mars of a balloon driven by means of a sixty horse-power engine. Mlle Garnerin, France's great *aeroporiste*, is the driver, or rather the pilot of this risky machine, which, one must hope, will not suffer the same fate as the Lennox balloon.' In 1846 in Antwerp he had been struck by the huge placards of a M. Kirsch pasted on the walls of the houses on the quay, and he had watched his balloon 'rising majestically towards evening, to the amazement of all the people, and then ignominiously grounded on the bank of a canal, or it might be in a potato field.' Gérard speculated that 'if one were ever to construct a balloon which could remain immobile above the earth's atmosphere, that is to say only twenty leagues above our heads, the aeronaut bold enough to make the experiment would find that time stopped for him. He would remain always at the same age and the same hour. . . . but there, no doubt, lies the secret of the immortality of the gods.'

However, he first became really interested in the subject on meeting in 1848 Félix Tournachon who was to become one of his most faithful friends. This strange character was introduced by Gérard to Alphonse Karr, for whose *Journal* they both worked assiduously. He was a giant of a man with huge legs and long arms, a shock of red hair, and lively, intelligent, frightened eyes. He came of a long family of printers which could be traced back to contemporaries of Gutenberg and Laurent Coster. With a dozen other volunteers he had taken part in a fantastic expedition to free Poland from Russo-German oppression. Neither he nor any of his companions knew a word of Polish, and they had difficulty in making the people understand the purpose of their expedition. All they actually achieved was the distinction of being taken prisoners of war for a few weeks.

He proved as conscientious a worker for the *Journal* as Gérard, and often the two of them spent the night sleeping on the printing tables. Like Turgan, Tournachon was keenly interested in balloons, but his own balloon, 'The Giant', collapsed as he was ascending and he himself was nearly killed. By turns writer, artist and poet, eventually in 1850 under the pseudonym of Nadar he opened a photographic studio in Paris and, in Aristide Marie's words, 'It is to him alone that we owe the preservation of the faithful image of him who tried so hard to remain unknown,' viz. Gérard de Nerval.

The failure of *Les Montenegrins* deprived Gérard of his expected remuneration but, ironically, the production brought him appreciation from an unexpected quarter. On 10 February 1850, he received a letter from a butcher in Montmartre asking, on behalf of the council of the Fat Ox of Montmartre, for permission to adopt the costumes for their festival and inviting him to visit his house on the occasion, 'where we shall have a little celebration among friends in costume and have a good time,' Gérard joined in with characteristic good will. But in his short speech he could not help revealing his Pythagorean convictions and, having told the assembled butchers that there was every chance of their being reincarnated as animals destined for slaughter, he took the opportunity of expressing a wish that the Fat Ox might be replaced by a Fat Bean. The butchers did not understand a word of his harangue, but they applauded vociferously. It was an occasion for enjoyment and they were flattered by the presence of an author.

Gérard's dissatisfaction with the Republic proceeded from a further recent disappointment. Under the pseudonym of Bosquillon he had written in collaboration with Méry another piece for the theatre, *La Nuit Blanche*, which was to have been produced at the Odéon. The setting was the court of King Soulouque who was proclaimed emperor of Haiti in 1849 and who was notorious for his stupidity, his vanity, and his cruelty. Certain verses appeared in the eyes of the censorship to satirize the French Government, and the piece was forbidden on the grounds of subversiveness.

Meanwhile another piece which Pierre Bocage, director of the Odéon, had requested towards the end of 1848, had been completed jointly with Méry and a third collaborator, the young Paul Bocage. This was *De Paris à Pekin*, a lavish production with elaborate scenery, ballets, chorus and music. Gérard, as optimistic as ever despite previous reversals, estimated that his share of the profits would amount to some ten thousand francs, and with this he planned to make a great journey to India and China.

It was to have succeeded at the Odéon *François le Champi*, which George Sand had adapted from her own novel. On the evening of the announcement, before an audience of fifteen hundred, Méry stepped on to the stage in front of the lowered curtain and began to read the programme in the form of a prologue in verse. But the 'drama in ten acts' was never to be played. The Théâtre National had been granted the exclusive privilege of producing musical dramas, and Bocage was forbidden to proceed with his. Determined nevertheless to make use of his elaborate and expensive scenery, he asked the disappointed authors for another piece for which the same sets could be used. Some years before Gérard had been fascinated by an Indian drama by Soudraka and had made a partial translation of it. Now this was resuscitated. Under the title of *Chariot d'Enfant* a complete translation in verse was quickly produced. It told the story of the redemption of a courtesan by her love for a poor Brahmin of high caste. Gérard worked at it exactingly, determined to ensure its success. But although, when it was produced on 13 May 1850, it had a good press, the exotic atmosphere of the drama with its flowery oriental language and the barbarous-sounding names of its characters met with an indifferent reception by the public, and it survived only a few performances.

The continual dashing of Gérard's highest hopes was bound sooner or later to have a cumulative effect on his excitable temperament. Constantly raised to a pitch of elation at the prospect of pecuniary success, only to be plunged again every time into the depths of disappointment and the old harassing struggle to earn his living, in June he experienced a period of severe nervous depression and once more submitted to the care of Dr Aussendon.

This, however, lasted no more than a few days, and he was soon at work collecting his impressions of Germany for the volume that was eventually to be published in 1852 under the title *Lorely*. On 15 August 1850 he left for Weimar, commissioned by François Buloz, editor of the *Revue des Deux Mondes* to write an account of the festivals celebrating the anniversaries of Herder and Goethe. Visiting on the way Cologne, Frankfurt (chiefly in order to view the house where Goethe was born), Cassal, Eisenach and the castle of Wartburg he was, characteristically, so delayed on the journey that he missed part of the programme, which began with a performance of Liszt's overture and choral settings for Herder's poem *Prometheus Freed*. He was however able to attend the first performance of *Lohengrin*, conducted by Liszt. Wagner's music was an entirely new experience for him, and he wrote an enthusiastic article for *La Presse* which greatly pleased the composer, not merely by its praise, but by the thorough understanding of his aims that it evinced.

Liszt had been entrusted with the organization of the festival. He and Gérard, who had remained good friends ever since their first meeting in Vienna, were happy to meet again. Together they visited Schiller's apartment, where Liszt's fingers touched the ancient spinet to life with Schubert's moving melody, 'Des Mädchens Klage'. It recalled to Gérard the beautiful princess in white dress and ermine cloak of whom he had caught a glimpse in Goethe's house in Weimar the day before, wandering 'among images of the past, like the divine Psyche representing life on a tombstone'. Only later, on his return to Paris, did he learn who she was when, in recognition of his articles on Weimar in the *Artiste,* he received from the hereditary grand-duke of Saxony, who had shown him over the ducal palace, a portrait of the young princess Marie of Prussia bearing a verse of Goethe's in his own hand.

After leaving Weimar Gérard went on to Leipzig and then back to Frankfurt and Brussels before returning to Paris on 21 September. There fresh vexations awaited him. He was attacked in an article in the *Corsaire* which accused him of being a turncoat and of expressing strong socialist views in *La Presse* whereas formerly he had been 'more royalist than the king' and had obtained missions under the July monarchy to subsidize his travels. Gérard took these accusations much to heart. He protested vigorously in both papers and in the *National,* even going so far as to assert that he had never had an official mission, which was of course untrue. He pointed out that the writer of the article had confused him with another Gérard. This was true but although, or perhaps because, he was never deeply interested in politics, the accusations were specious enough.

Before the end of the year he was confronted with a further harassment in the form of a notice of eviction from his lodging in the Rue Saint Thomas du Louvre. Humble as it was, he had a sentimental affection for it, as being in the neighbourhood of the former Rue du Doyenné. Now the last of the buildings in this area were to be pulled down 'for the reconstruction of the surroundings of the Louvre and the extension of the Rue de Rivoli'. In order that 'the expenses occasioned by this eviction in the interests of public utility' should not be at the charge of the tenant, he was granted a sum of twenty francs which, he was informed, he could claim at any time within a fortnight. The expropriation, Gérard considered, was perfectly justified, but the compensation totally inadequate and he never claimed it.

11

The Illuminati

In the autumn of 1850 Gérard undertook a serial contribution to the *National*, which began to appear in October under the title *Les Faux Saulniers*; such was the name given to the salt-smugglers who, under the old regime, had operated in the north and east of France. The story presented the picaresque history of one Archembault de Bucquoy. It tells of his arrest at Senlis in mistake for another man suspected of fomenting trouble and supporting the contrabandists, and of his subsequent successive imprisonments and escapes, in the last instance from the Bastille.

On his return to Paris Gérard had found literature 'in a state of inexpressible dismay'. Already under the Tinguy Act, every composition in the form of a novel was subject to an extra stamp duty but now, with the recent promulgation of the Riancey Amendment 'journals were forbidden to insert what the assembly is pleased to call the *serial novel*. I have seen a number of writers, of no political colour whatever, in despair at this decision which struck a cruel blow at their means of existence. . . . I am beginning to be frightened now at the sentences awaiting journals for the least infraction of the text of the new law. Fifty francs fine for every copy seized is something to make the most intrepid recoil : for, as far as those journals are concerned which have a circulation of no more than twenty-five thousand at most – and there are several of them – that would amount to more than a million. It can be seen then how a broad interpretation of the law would place in the hands of power the means of extinguishing all opposition.'

In mockery of the law he adopted for his story a method of narration admirably suited to his temperament, interweaving in his account endless digressions and commentaries, very much in the manner of Sterne. The result is a curious combination of historical fact, fancy, reminiscence, comment and divagation sometimes carried to excess, that nevertheless contains some of his most sincere and affecting writing.

He tells how in Frankfurt he had chanced to find in a second-hand bookshop a copy of the *Histoire du sieur abbé comte de*

Bucquoy. Finding it of great interest, he leafed through it but the price demanded was too high and he thought he would easily obtain a copy in Paris or be able to find it in a library. The book proved more elusive than he had supposed, but in the course of his search he came on a manuscript containing the history of de Bucquoy's great-aunt, Angelique de Longueval, which he also recounts. Significantly his researches led him back to the Ile de France – to Compiègne, Soissons, Senlis, Chantilly, Châalis. Amid the melancholy splendour of autumn he wandered again through the villages – Pontarmé, Dammartin, La Chapelle en Serval, Montagny, Othys, Mortefontaine – and memories of his childhood were again reawakened, to be incorporated in the story of *Angélique.*

Later in 1852, *Les Faux Saulniers* was split up, some parts being embodied in the *Bohème Galante* and others in *Lorely.* The story of Angélique was included in the *Filles du Feu,* which was published in 1854, and that of de Bucquoy formed a chapter of *Les Illuminés* of 1852.

Although the six stories or studies comprising it are of unequal interest, *Les illuminés ou les précurseurs de socialisme* is a key work for the understanding of Nerval. Not only are all the usual Nervalian themes and preoccupations developed in it, but the man himself is discovered and the origin of much of his mystical thinking revealed. The ideas and speculations that had occupied him among the Druses and elsewhere during his eastern journey had not ceased to interest him and, as naturally as his researches into the history of the de Bucquoys and the Longuevals, these too recalled him to the country of his childhood, in particular to Ermenonville, that retreat of occultism in the eighteenth century, where the great Illuminati had gathered regularly.

The work is not strictly confined to the Illuminati. Its six sections, all of which had previously appeared in periodicals between 1839 and 1850, are studies of eccentrics. The first of these is *Le Roi de Bicêtre,* Raoul Spifume, the King of Bedlam, who in the sixteenth century, on account of his extraordinary resemblance to Henry II, deceived himself into believing that he was the king. The story, in which Maquet collaborated, is chiefly of interest because it exemplifies two of Gérard's favourite themes, that of the double or Sosie[1] and that of 'the spilling-over of dream into real life'. Thus we read of Spifume that 'at night he was robbed of his real existence by extraordinary dreams, and he assumed an altogether different

---

[1] The name is taken from Molière's *Amphytrion,* in which Mercury impersonates Amphytrion's servant, Sosie.

identity.' Confined in a madhouse he became convinced that 'his dreams were his real life and that his confinement was only a dream.' It is almost as if Gérard was foretelling his own experience in 1841, two years after the story was written.

The story of the seventeenth-century Abbé du Bucquoy has already been mentioned. The rest of the gallery consists of portraits of eighteenth-century characters. The study of Cagliostro, which first appeared in the *Almanach Cabalistique* in 1850, provided Gérard with an opportunity to expound theosophical theories drawn from such cabbalistic writers as the Abbé de Villars, Father Bougeant and Dom Pernety. He explains how there developed a 'half-religious and half-philosophical school of thought which, doubtless abounding in heresies, but frequently accepted or tolerated by the catholic clergy, maintained a certain spirit of mysticism or supernaturalism essential to thoughtful and sensitive imaginations.' This leads him to consider the prolonged contact of Christianity with the East during the crusades and the evolution of the Templars, who 'in the desire to establish a bond between their order and the Syrian peoples whom they were entrusted to govern, laid the foundations of a sort of new dogma which partook of all the religions practised by the Levantines, without abandoning fundamentally the catholic synthesis.' From the Templars he traces the rise of the Freemasons towards the end of the seventeenth century and their attempt to establish a system of universal morality in an age of increasing scepticism and materialism. So, by way of the Rosicrucians, the Martinists and the Swedenborgians Gérard leads up to the Illuminati, the sect originally founded by Weisshaupt in Germany in 1776, whose republican ideas paved the way for the later exponents of socialism.

Whether Gérard himself was a Freemason is doubtful. Certainly he was very well informed on the rites of secret societies in Germany, which he had studied when engaged on *Léo Burckart* and which were closely related to those of Freemasonry. The majority of his friends and acquaintances were Freemasons, and on more than one occasion he professed to be an initiate. In the *Voyage en Orient* he writes, 'I have produced my titles, luckily having among my papers one of those beautiful Masonic diplomas full of cabbalistic signs familiar to the Orientals.' The statement may be pure fantasy, and the declaration made in a letter to Dr Blanche, by which he would seem to have entered the brotherhood in 1847, is wholly unreliable owing to the mentally deranged tone of the letter. In any case, even if the initiation he sought was of an altogether different and higher order, the fact remains that he was deeply interested in the secret rites of Freemasonry.

Both as a Freemason, then, and as an alchemist, the strange figure of Giuseppe Balsamo, the self-styled Count Cagliostro, had a natural appeal for Gérard, particularly since he had attended the famous suppers at Ermenonville. Cagliostro's recognition of Isis as a supreme divinity found a ready response in Gérard, as also his theory that there are no dead. 'His wife, who was very lovely and very intelligent, had accompanied him on all his travels. She presided at that famous supper, which was attended by most of the philosophers of that time and at which several persons recently dead were made to appear. . . . Twelve places were laid, although only six had been invited : d'Alembert, Diderot, Voltaire, the Duke of Choiseul, the Abbé de Voisenon, and someone else, took their places, although they were dead, and conversed with the guests *de omni re scibili, et quibusdam aliis.*'[1]

Cagliostro had met the Count Saint Germain in Germany and been initiated by him. Saint Germain, alchemist and seer, was one of the most curious and colourful characters among the Illuminati. It was he who 'showed Louis XV the fate of his children in a magic mirror, and the king recoiled in horror on seeing the image of the dauphin appear decapitated.' He 'professed to have preserved the memory of a host of previous existences, and recounted his various adventures since the beginning of the world.'

In Jacques Cazotte Gérard discovered a still more sympathetic character. His study of the author of the *Diable Amoureux*, which had originally appeared as an introduction to an illustrated edition of that book in 1845, clearly shows that he had much in common with his subject and shared or adopted many of his views. 'This man,' he says, 'who was to begin with a graceful poet of the school of Marot and La Fontaine, then a simple story-teller, fascinated now by the colour of the old French tales in verse, now by the lively sparkle of oriental stories brought into vogue by the success of the *Thousand and One Nights*, . . . surrendered himself to the most terrible danger of the literary life, that of taking his own inventions seriously,' and he describes him as 'a poet whom love of the marvellous purely as allegory, led little by little to the most sincere and ardent mysticism.' It was exactly Gérard's own case.

But it is Cazotte's mystical theories that coincide most closely with Gérard's own. 'We all live', he said, 'among the spirits of our fathers; the invisible world presses about us on every side.' Cazotte's inability at times to distinguish between the living and the dead was an experience almost identical with Gérard's in the

[1] On every known topic and other things besides.

hallucinatory dreams he describes in *Aurélia*. Like Cazotte, Gérard believed in 'the necessity of human action to establish communication between heaven and earth', that is, between the material world of men and the outer world of spirits. After quoting at length Cazotte's account of a dream he had in 1791, Gérard says, 'In this care to recover a dream which was partly devoid of sense, one need see only the preoccupations of a mystic who connects the phenomena of sleep with the activity of the exterior world.' It is, in fact just such preoccupations that are the initial cause of 'the spilling-over of dream into reality'.

But of all these characters, it was in Nicolas, Restif de la Bretonne that Gérard found the clearest and most faithful reflection of himself. Indeed the resemblances between the two are so striking as almost to make one wonder momentarily whether Gérard's life was not consciously modelled on Restif's. It is for this reason that the section of the book entitled 'Les Confidences de Nicolas', which first appeared in the *Revue des Deux Mondes* in 1850 and which is the longest in the book, is also by far the most successful. Gérard understood Restif through himself and in these pages he brings him to life with a skill so far unequalled in his other stories.

Like Gérard, in his childhood Restif wandered about his native countryside, in his case the Bourgogne, in company with his playmates, young girls such as Marie and Madeleine. One day in church he first caught sight of Jeanette Rousseau, with whom he immediately fell in love, recognizing in her his ideal of beauty. Jeanette is the counterpart of Gérard's Adrienne and has the same religious connotations. Many years later Restif wrote, 'I did everything in order to be worthy of that girl, whose name makes me tremble at sixty, after forty-six years without seeing her.' Adrienne was several years older than Gérard, Jeanette three years older than Restif. And just as Gérard saw in Jenny and others the reincarnation of Adrienne, so Restif had seen in Madame Paragon and Zéfire the features of his first love, Jeanette. There was also of course Mlle Guéant, the young actress of the Comédie-Française, the exact counterpart of Gérard's Jenny Colon.

'The theory of resemblances', Gérard says, 'is one of Restif's favourite ideas.' In the same passage he declares that it is scarcely possible to admit, as Restif claims, that he had 'always loved the same woman . . . in three separate persons'. Yet this was precisely what Gérard claimed for himself. It was a love 'for an image that I had created in my own mind, for a fantasy, fugitive as a dream, which I did not even think of realizing, for one of those impossibilities which I have pursued all my life and which I do not know what destiny has sometimes rendered possible.' Is it Gérard or Restif speaking? 'I loved you in a different way; I loved you as one loves those strange visions that one sees in dreams, so clearly that one awakes captivated by a noble passion, faint memory of the impressions of youth . . . at which one laughs a moment later! . . . Am I quite sure myself that I have been in love? The daytime images are for me like the visions of the night! Woe to any who enters my eternal dream without being an impalpable figure!' Restif, we are told, 'like all proud spirits always believed in some fate which, relatively to him alone, took the place of chance'. The same belief governed Gérard's whole life, so that he was always watching for signs and numbers that would reveal his destiny. He believed that 'the hour of our birth, the spot on the earth where we appeared, the first gesture, the name, the room – and all those consecrations, and all those rites that are imposed on us, all this establishes a happy or a fatal sequence on which the entire future depends.'

We may point to one final similarity between them. In the second part of his account Gérard writes, 'For a long time now, Nicolas had been living alone, speaking to nobody, working all day, and in the evening wandering at random through the deserted streets,' and later he relates how Restif grew old, always more and more morose, oppressed by money losses and by private troubles. 'His only communication with the world was to go in the evening to the Café Manoury, where he sometimes discussed politics and philosophy in a loud voice. . . . Usually he sat in a corner and played chess until eleven o'clock in the evening. At that time, whether the game was finished or not, he rose silently and went out, . . . to wander along the embankments, above all around the Cité and the Ile Saint Louis, *whatever the weather might be*; he plunged into the muddy streets of the crowded districts, and returned home only when he had made a good harvest of observations on the disorderly and bloody scenes which he had witnessed. Often he intervened in these obscure dramas, and played Don Quixote to persecuted innocence or vanquished feebleness. Sometimes he operated by persuasion; sometimes, too, his authority was due to a suspicion that he was acting for the police.'

Gérard who, at forty-five, contemplating his ravaged face in a mirror, sadly and fancifully evolved a fresh derivation of his name from the Greek $\gamma\eta\rho\alpha s$ (old age), was then living much the same sort of life. His existence was becoming more and more solitary as he withdrew further into the visionary world of his imagination. Though he did not play chess, in his own corner of the café he occupied himself with his writing, and after nightfall he would roam about the city, often in the more squalid quarters. He mixed with all types and perhaps deserved as much as Restif the sobriquet of 'the Jean Jacques of the markets'. Moreover, as will appear, the passage on Restif quoted above, might be taken to have some bearing on the tragedy of Gérard's death.

In his final study, in *Les Illuminés*, of Quintus Aucler, the last of the Pagans, Gérard attempts a resolution of the conflict within himself of philosophy and religion. His personal anguish is clearly illustrated when he writes, 'There is, most certainly, something more frightening in history than the fall of empires; it is the death of religions. . . . The true believer can escape this feeling, but, subject to the scepticism of our age, one trembles at finding so many gloomy doors opening on nothingness.' In Aucler's syncretism he finds some satisfaction. 'If the barbarians had understood that the new god which they were imposing by the sword was no other than *Chris-na,* the Indian Bacchus – that is to say the third Bacchus of the Eleusinian Mysteries, who was called Iacchus, to distinguish him from Dionysus and Zagreus, his brothers! – But they could not recognize in their god the favourite of Ceres, the Ιησους crowned with vines – and without concerning themselves with the symbol, they kept only the consecratory rite of the bread and wine; all ignorant – the barbarians like the Fathers of the Church – other barbarians, whose simple works have been rewritten by hired sophists.' Gérard finds in Aucler's neo-paganism an expression of pantheism, and in his 'revival of the ideas of the school of Alexandria' support for his favourite theories of the transmigration of souls and the planetary influence over human destinies.

12

The Double

The year 1851 opened with every prospect of success and recognition, for not only was his Faustian drama *L'Imagier de Harlem* almost completed, but in January Gérard entered into an agreement with the publisher Charpentier for the definitive edition of the *Voyage en Orient*. He intended it to be a work of permanent literary value, to be compared for style and originality with those of Chateaubriand and Lamartine. The two volumes appeared in June, but in the meantime the original journalistic pieces required a great deal of revision, rewriting and intercalation to convert them into a unified work of literature. Gérard set about the task with characteristic enthusiasm, but he was hard-pressed for time and in March we find him protesting in a letter to Charpentier, 'I have never been behindhand with copy . . . the first volume has been done fairly quickly and in fact I have scarcely worked on anything else for the last two months. You would surely wish to have a carefully prepared work and one worthy of survival rather than that it should be ready some days earlier than this would allow. However I believe we shall have few difficulties now. But I have done everything conscientiously and have been to the printers every day, except when there was nothing to be done there. Besides you know that there is always a tendency to blame the author.'

As soon as the edition was ready, Gérard busied himself with other tasks. Some years before he had spoken to Houssaye of Kotzebue and his *Misanthropy and Repentance*; now at the request of Houssaye, who had become the director of the Comédie Française, he had undertaken to translate and adapt the piece. He was finding it 'very difficult, more difficult than I thought, not to understand but to render; this old-style German resists the French as much as possible.'

He was at the same time negotiating with a publisher for the book on the Illuminati, and was engaged on the article on Quintus Aucler for the *Revue de Paris* when, on the evening of 24 September he went to dine with a friend, Rigo, at his house in Montmartre. Together they watched the sunset from a raised terrace which commanded an extensive view. On the way down Gérard tripped and fell down the steps, striking his chest on a sharp corner, badly bruising himself, and spraining a knee. Evidently, too, he suffered from shock. He thought at first that he had received a mortal blow, but, recovering after a little, he was able to drag himself home to bed. Next day he wrote to Maxime du Camp with regard to the article on Aucler, 'Just now it is a question of more than a delay; I have had an accident from which I nearly died and from which I shall perhaps suffer permanent effects. Don't laugh, I beg you; for me at least it is very serious. I was getting on well, I had nearly a half-folio and I should have finished the whole tomorrow at the latest.'

In its physical effects the accident was not as serious as he supposed, but he was in a low state and, combined with the nervous tension induced by the strain of overwork, it disturbed him profoundly. Although *Aurélia* is not to be taken as an exact case-history, his account of the occasion therein suggests that his mental condition at the time may have been partly responsible for his fall. In it he relates that on his way to Rigo's he chanced to pass a house where he heard a bird 'talking', and took this for an evil augury. The bird reminded him of another which he had encountered a long time before in one of his hallucinatory visions and which had seemed to him to speak with the voice of one of his dead relatives.

Birds played a significant part in the Nervalian mythology. The hoopoe, for example, which was a bird of augury among the Arabs, was the agent of recognition between Adoniram and Balkis, the Queen of Sheba, in the *Voyage en Orient*, and it appears again in the triumphal conclusion to *Aurélia*. Here the hoopoe is represented as possessing a sort of mystical intelligence which functions on behalf of human beings. To Gérard the fact that a bird could utter human words, however incoherently, seemed to imply some mysterious form of communication with the spirits of the 'outer' world, and he would waste hours in visits to a pet-shop near his lodgings where there was a magnificent parrot with which he held long conversations. Like Baudelaire he was an admirer of Edgar Allan Poe, whose 'Raven' in particular fascinated him.[1] Was it, one wonders, the raven that haunted the steps of the lodging-house in the Rue de la Vieille Lanterne that drew him to that sordid alley on the night he died?

Slight as were the injuries resulting from his accident, Gérard was nevertheless ill until the end of November. It is probable that

---

[1] See footnote p. 141.

during this period he stayed with Dr Emile Blanche, the son of Dr Esprit Blanche, who had treated him before but who had recently died. This was the Dr Emile Blanche who in these last years of Gérard's life was to become his most sympathetic professional attendant and friend.

If we are to believe the account of this illness given in *Aurélia* – and the general tone is convincingly authentic – on returning home he became 'feverish' (it is the term he usually employs to describe the state of mental disorder) and, suddenly recalling that the terrace from which he had admired the sunset overlooked the cemetery where Jenny Colon was buried, he began to fancy that some subconscious awareness of the fact might have been responsible for his fall. From this, in his pain and despondency, it was but a step further to wish that fate had intervened with a sterner hand so that death might have reunited him with her. But then, reconsidering the life he had led since her death, he began to reproach himself 'not with having forgotten her, for that I had not done, but with having outraged her memory by indulging in casual love-affairs'. He was not worthy of her, he concluded.

It was then that it occurred to him to seek assurance in dream, but he was dismayed to find that 'her image, which had often appeared to me in my dreams, returned no more.' Instead he encountered only his 'double' whom he had first encountered after his first violent outbreak in 1841, and who had already threatened him in a previous hallucinatory dream or vision. Now this same figure seemed to attack him with a weapon whose shape he was unable to distinguish. The horror came when he recognized him. 'It was my own face, it was my own form idealized and grown taller.' He was immediately reminded of 'that mystical brother whom the Orientals call Ferouer', and was persuaded that every man comprises two distinct personalities, identical in appearance, one being the good and the other the evil genius. Which was he? In any case the two are mutually hostile, and he must fight to the end. In his delirium he comes upon a mansion in which a marriage has been prepared. It is his double who is to obtain Aurélia. He bursts in to prevent the catastrophe, and again he is held off, this time more specifically by a man 'carrying a long bar tipped with a red-hot ball'. The unconscious symbolism of Gérard's dreams has long since become apparent, and his fear of impotence is clearly indicated in this incident. Yet now he is more concerned with his eventual union with the mother-bride-goddess figure in whom finally are to be combined Adrienne-Aurélia, his lost mother, Isis, and the Virgin Mary. He is already orientated towards the supernatural world of planetary spirits. There he feels he has command.

He knows the sign that has magical power to subdue his antagonists. He raises his arm in triumph, when suddenly a woman's cry of heart-rending grief breaks out through the night to recall him to reality. But no one has cried out, he is told upon enquiry. Nevertheless he is still convinced that it was a real cry that he heard. If it did not sound in the material world about him, then it must have echoed from that world of spirits beyond, and he had caused it. What had he done? By striving to penetrate the secrets of that mysterious existence he had 'disturbed the harmony of the magic universe from which my soul had derived the certainty of an immortal existence.' He fancied that perhaps he was cursed for having offended against the divine law and 'must expect only anger and contempt for ever'.

Previously he had succeeded in convincing himself of the certainty of attaining his ideal, Aurélia, in that other world beyond death, but now in the depression caused by his mental and physical debility he was seized with fear of losing her in that world too. It seemed to him that some guilt of his must have brought this fate upon him and that his only hope lay in expiation.

In these strange and terrible dreams can be clearly traced an extension of ideas drawn from his study of Quintus Aucler with which he had been occupied at the time when his accident occurred. The coincidence of events in the material and supernatural worlds is exemplified in his realization that the blow he received in his fall was at the same time a blow struck by his double with the weapon he held in his hand, and also in his firm belief, in spite of the evidence, that the cry of the woman sounding in his dream had been a real one. Again dream and reality had become indistinguishable, and when his dearest friends came to see him and condole with him 'there was a double meaning in everything these people said to me, although they were unaware of it, since they did not exist *in the spirit* as I did.'

Yet, although the symptoms were all of precisely the same nature, he was at pains to assure his friends that he had not suffered a return of his former mental illness. 'You know', he wrote to Maxime du Camp, 'that when one falls from a height of two feet and with one's whole weight on the corner of a stove [*sic*] and on one's left breast, when moreover one sprains one's knee, and when for two whole days every time one breathes it feels as if an arrow pierces one's chest, one cannot be sure that there is not some internal lesion. Today I am reassured and there is no more talk of sending me to a nursing-home. Théophile saw me so bruised and so upset that I am afraid he may have frightened you.'

A month after his recovery, on 27 December, *L'Imagier de*

Harlem was produced at the Porte Saint Martin. Gérard had long dreamed of achieving a Faust of his own, but with a French flavour, and without imitating Goethe. As early as 1838 he had discussed the possibility of such a project with Dumas, to be based on the legends of which Goethe had made no use. Over the years he had sketched several drafts of the work, which was to be his masterpiece. Now in collaboration with Méry, since Dumas was away from France, he had completed it.

The play was intended to show the difficulties with which the first inventors of printing had to contend in order to establish their ideas, but it was also to be fundamentally religious in design, like a mystery play of the Middle Ages, showing that Providence favours enlightenment and progress which the Devil would like to suppress. Of the two women in the inventor's story one, Catherine, is the homely type from whose lack of understanding he suffers but whose religious sensibility saves him in the end, and the other is the ideal woman, the eternal dream of genius, symbolized in Goethe's *Faust* by Helen. Here she is Alilah or Lilith, the woman eternally damned whom the Devil uses to seduce all great men in order to frustrate their aims. Instead of Faust or Gutenberg, Laurent Coster was chosen as protagonist because, few details of his life being known, the authors had more scope in adapting it to their requirements. Marc Fournier seems to have spared nothing in the lavish production of this drama in five acts and ten scenes, which incorporated a ballet with music by Alphonse Degroot.

In a letter to his friend, Jules Janin, just before the first performance Gérard drew his attention to the production and appealed to him in these words, 'The success of the piece will do me less good than its failure will do me harm. That is why I recall to you our long and constant friendship.' Unluckily, for some unaccountable reason Janin, who long afterwards declared, 'I gave him every possible help,' in his report in the *Journal des Débats* complained that the theatre was too cold and damned the piece as being written in 'good prose and bad verse'. The public reception, however, was at first favourable, and Gérard, believing success assured, demonstrated his satisfaction by distributing presents among the actors. To Marie Laurent, who played the part of Alilah, he gave a bracelet costing four hundred francs, which he borrowed from Méry. Once again he felt free to travel.

But on 23 January 1852, Méry received a letter from Marc Fournier in which he stated that for a fortnight the play had been running at a loss; every performance now represented a deficit of two hundred francs, and it would have to be withdrawn. When Méry showed the letter to Gérard, he 'read it and clasped his head in his hands as though to prevent his reason escaping. Then his face contracted in a nerve-strained laugh, while his eyes retained a sombre sadness and filled with tears.'

On the same day Gérard entered the Municipal Hospital in the Faubourg St Denis, the Maison Dubois. For some time he had been unwell. On 6 January he had appealed to his faithful friend Stadler who had taken him home and given him his own bed and, with the help of Nadar, watched over him when a doctor they called in diagnosed fever. The official diagnosis was erysipelas, but one is reminded of the purpureal fever to which he had almost succumbed in his childhood. There can be little doubt that throughout his life he was subject to attacks of this sort, which in their milder form frequently passed unnoticed. As Méry observed, the continual alternation of hopeful elation and disillusioned despondency was too much for him to bear. He had not the constitution to combat repeated misfortune.

By 15 February he was well enough to leave the Maison Dubois and take up his affairs again. He was principally occupied with the publication of his *Illuminés*, the *Petits Châteaux de Bohème*, and *Lorely*. At the same time he was engaged in ceaseless efforts to get his friend Stadler's verse drama, the *Bois de Daphne*, accepted. It was a noteworthy characteristic of Gérard that, even when his own fortune was at its lowest ebb, he would readily exert himself on behalf of his friends.

A new project, too, was on hand as the result of a conversation with Hippolyte Lucas, in the course of which they had discussed the possibility of producing a new poetic drama to fit the music of *Die Zauberflöte*. Lucas had written a piece entitled *Aurore*, which Gérard suggested could suitably be combined with an old manuscript of his own, the story of Francesco and Polia. This had never ceased to interest him, and in the rough outline of the proposed work that he sketched for Lucas the familiar theme of the resemblance between one woman and another appears again. It was the very subject, one might suppose, to call forth his best efforts, but nothing came of the suggested collaboration. Perhaps he realized at last that he had all along been wasting his talent in his dramatic writings and that he had in fact no gift for the theatre.

In expectation of a great success for *L'Imagier de Harlem*, Gérard had spent money recklessly. Now, once again reduced to the necessity of severe economy, he was lodging in the Rue du Mail. Alfred Busquet, whom he took one day to visit his apartment, was surprised when, on entering, the porter solemnly handed Gérard a bedroom candlestick. They went up two floors and entered a large bare room containing only a bed in an alcove and a dozen flour sacks stuffed full leaning against the wall. 'There is my bed,' said Gérard, and, pointing to the sacks, 'There is my library. Would you like it? . . . I will give it you.' He was willing now to relinquish even these long-treasured possessions.

As before in such circumstances Gérard's one recourse was to travel. Temporarily recovered as he was, his friends were still uneasy about him. On 7 May Théo, writing to Ernesta Grisi who was then in Constantinople, said, 'Gérard has left for Copenhagen in a state of mind that is scarcely reassuring but physically healed at least to all appearance.' In fact he went not to Copenhagen but to Brussels, where he was to join Houssaye for a journey in Holland. At Dumas's he found Noel Parfait who with many others, among them Victor Hugo, had been exiled from France on 9 January. Here, in spite of the atmosphere of dejection caused by the expulsion order, Gérard was warmly welcomed, and indeed was well received everywhere as on his previous visits, for he had many friends in the city. A little later, on reaching Antwerp, he wrote in a letter to Stadler, 'You will no doubt be surprised to see that I have only come as far as this. But I stopped everywhere on my way, notably at Brussels, where they fed me too well. Today I have put myself on a diet of smoked herring, because before leaving Brussels this morning I suffered a beefsteak at 92 centimes. They are better at Véry's for 75; still it is the only culinary expense my stay has cost me, but as for the rest!'

On 21 May he wrote to his father, telling him of his visits to the Hague, Amsterdam, and Zaandam, or Saardam as he calls it, describing it as 'an enchanting town which has retained the Chinese look of the old Dutch towns, which they begin to lose nearer to us'. He continues, 'I have drunk no more than a half-bottle of wine during the whole of my stay, considering that the ordinary wine costs four francs a bottle, and even then one can hardly tell whether it is wine or wild-cherry juice slightly fermented,' and concludes, 'I cannot delay my return, for I have no more on me than 250 francs, and that goes quickly when it is changed into florins.' But the journey had been worthwhile in one respect at least, for in the same letter he writes, 'I am extremely well; the journey and the change of air have restored not only my health, but my youth. It was what I needed after my illness.'

On the other hand he had written nothing, and on his return he retired to write up the journey in peace. The result was an article on the May festivals in Holland which appeared in the *Revue des Deux Mondes* in June, but naturally the payment for this went but a very little way towards defraying his travelling expenses and, although both *Lorely* and *Les Illuminés* were due to appear soon, the customary struggle for existence continued.

In August he visited again the Ile de France, preparing the setting for his new story, *Sylvie*. He was still occupied with this in October when he went back once more to renew his inspiration in the misty landscapes of his loved Valois. In a letter to Buloz, the editor of the *Revue des Deux Mondes,* he wrote, 'I have found some good things, and it is developing well. As far as I am concerned it is finished, that is to say written in pencil on a quantity of scraps of paper, so that I have only to rewrite it: three or four days of fresh determined effort,' but in the meantime he was forced to write other articles in order to keep going, and he added, 'I very much doubt whether it will be ready by the end of the month; but it is *better,* isn't it, that it should be *better.*'

His fragmentary method of composition at this time is described by his friend and collaborator, Méry: 'Gérard de Nerval worked slowly and as the inspiration came to him. His writing-desk was inclined to be anywhere; he would write on a milestone like Mercier or on a café table, never at home; his coat pockets were stuffed with little squares of paper and he often lost his best periods. When the sun tempted him to walk in the country, he would set off to wander about the suburb, pencil in hand, writing, sometimes quite illegibly, all the charming things with which the freshness of spring inspired him. Afterwards he had to put so many scattered little pages in order, correct the mistakes of improvization, check an idea of dubious veracity, perfect the style as much as possible, and pay a copyist so as to be able to present an acceptable whole to the printer. The fresh work of revision had to be done on this first copy; fresh work, too, for the copyist and additional expense.' As Gérard himself said, it was only the need for haste that made him work, 'otherwise I *polish* too much'.

Lorely, Souvenirs d'Allemagne was published in August, but he received only 150 francs for the first edition. As the year drew to a close, in the face of dwindling resources, he began to fear the harshness of the approaching winter. Eleven years before, finding himself in the same position after recovering from his first serious mental illness, he had applied for help to Auguste Cave of the Ministry of the Interior, at the same time enlisting the support of his friend Louis Perrot, who had entered the ministry in 1835 as examiner of dramatic works. Cave had died in March 1852, and so Gérard now appealed again to Perrot:

My dear friend, don't forget what I told you; a leg up would save me this winter, and I should be profoundly grateful for it. I would not dream of making such an application, I who have worked for twelve years without asking for any help; but, having been so dangerously ill last winter, the prospect of a return, with the bad weather, of a certain state of health which demands a little rest and care frightens me.

You know that it was overwork that endangered me and since then I have again written a great deal. I have published two books : *Les Illuminés* and *Lorely*, and articles in the reviews.

If what I ask could be supplied from the funds for the encouragement of dramatic art, my titles to it are two light operas : *Piquillo* and *Les Montenegrins,* and three big dramas : *Léo Burckart, Le Chariot d'Enfant,* and *L'Imagier,* with which the Porte Saint Martin reopened.

If it is a matter of the funds for literature, you know that I have to write for Furne a description of travels in the Mediterranean for which I have been chosen as being the author of the *Voyage en Orient* published by Charpentier. I have to begin in March and I must prepare beforehand. Do your best to make my motives clear and to explain how unused I am to making requests. I believe I am only asking for what could be less well spent, considering the need to take care of my health and my certainty of being able subsequently to apply myself to useful works.

I trust you to speak for me, you who helped me so much when I was ill this year.

It must have cost him dear to write such a letter, he who all his life had struggled so hard to preserve his independence. Yet even at this time of misery and depression he could still think of others, as witness his letter to Madame de Solms on 2 January 1853.

Gérard's relations with Madame de Solms remain an obscure episode in his life. Marie Laetitia Studholme Wyse, princesse de Solms, was born at Waterford in Ireland on 25 April 1833, the daughter of Sir Thomas Wyse, MP, and Laetitia Buonaparte. At fifteen she was married to Frederic de Solms. After the death of her husband she married Count Ratazzi in 1863. Two years later she was expelled from France on the publication of her *Mariages de la Créole,* and went to live near Florence. Ratazzi died in 1873, and in 1877 she married Luiz de Rute, a former deputy and Secretary of State in Spain. She was at that time a very beautiful young woman and is said to have had innumerable lovers, especially among men of letters. She was so eager to be known and talked about that she seems almost to have welcomed scandal; Alphonse Karr ironically nicknamed her the 'Princesse Brouhaha'. Gérard on the other hand, was obviously entranced by her. Was she, perhaps, yet another incarnation of Adrienne? In any case he was on sufficiently intimate terms with her to apply to her with confidence to relieve the misery of a family whom he had by chance encountered in his wanderings.

Do not give me, dear beneficent fairy, the beautiful book you promised me for a New Year gift; I have coveted those beautiful gilt-edged volumes for a very long time. But they will cost too much and I have something better to propose to you : a good deed. I can feel you tremble with joy, you whose heart is always so hungry. Well now, here is something, my lovely friend, with which to occupy it for a whole week! Rue St Jacques, No. 7, on the fifth floor, sunk in frightful misery – unspeakable misery – father, mother, seven children, out of work, without fire, without bread, without light.

Two of the children are half-dead with hunger. One of those chances by which I am often guided took me there yesterday. I gave them all I had : my cloak and forty centimes. What a mere nothing! Then I told them that a great lady, a fairy, a queen seventeen years old would come to their wretched lodging with everything complete, gold coins, blankets, bread for the children. They looked at me as if I had gone mad. I really believe I promised them rubies and diamonds, and these poor people did not quite understand, but they began to smile and cry.

Ah! If you could have seen them! Quick, then, run to them, with your great soft eyes which will make them believe an angel is appearing, to fulfil what your poor poet has promised in your name. Devote to this good work the money you would have spent on my New Year present, for I positively want to contribute towards it, or better still remit by D— the eighty francs which the beautiful work I no longer wish to think of must have cost, and I will run to the Temple and to old Verdureau's to buy everything fit to set up a Russian prince on holiday.

It will be lovely, you will see! You will be dazzled! I will run to Béranger's to search. Goodbye for the present, little queen, I hope to see you soon in *our* paupers' attic. Our paupers! I am proud to be able to write these words. There is, then, someone poorer than I – according to the world's decree. Don't forget the number. On the fifth floor, second passage, the door on the left.

Good-bye, Darling, dear Darling, sweet Darling, providence of the afflicted, darling Darling, so charming and so delicate, so devoid of pride and so kind! Wear your dress with the long train and your high-heeled shoes! I have promised them a great princess, large as life, more powerful than all earthly powers. They won't believe it any more when they see you at seventeen with your fresh young smile. But I am joking, I am joking; good-bye, darling, good-bye once more. – Forgive me, madam.

4   Rousseau's tomb at Ermenonville

5   The ruins of Châalis Abbey

6   Rue de la Vieille Lanterne
Photo Bulloz

13

The Thread of Ariadne

Gérard's depression deepened as the winter advanced. Fear of ill-health and of a recurrence of his previous mental disorder, of a second descent into Hell as he termed it, the continual nagging necessity of working against time, anxiety about fulfilling his commitments, and above all the dread of creative impotence, all combined to drive him to the brink of despair. The gloomiest thoughts possessed him. At first, believing Aurélia stolen by his double and so lost to him for all eternity, he had had a moment of revolt : 'I will fight against the fatal spirit,' he had told himself, 'I will fight against God himself with the weapons of tradition and learning. Whatever he may do in the darkness and the night, I exist, and to defeat him I have all the time that is yet given me to live on earth.'

But now he found himself utterly unworthy. He had repudiated God. He had committed the error, imputed by St Augustine to the Manichees, of 'choosing to worship and serve a creature rather than the Creator'. He had made a god of his love and worshipped in pagan fashion her whose last breath had been consecrated to Christ. His one ray of hope seemed to lie in making reparation. 'If', he argued, 'there is any truth in this religion, God can still pardon me. He can give her back to me, if I humble myself before him; perhaps her spirit will return to me!' In this mood of self-abasement, reviewing his past, for all his innate docility and altruism, he saw his life as one 'madly dissipated in which evil has very often triumphed'.

One day he came upon a funeral procession going to the cemetery in Montmartre where Jenny was buried, and followed it. In his conviction of the intimate relation between the spiritual and material worlds which enabled the dead to see and hear the living, he thought that the stranger whose coffin he was following would perhaps be made happier by the sympathy of 'a brother in grief, sadder than any of the others who were accompanying him'. The thought brought tears to his eyes and suddenly, like Coleridge's Ancient Mariner when he blessed the water-snakes, he felt that he could pray. This seemed to him a sign of the promise of salvation and he was filled with joy.

The cemetery he had entered was sacred to him as the burial-place not only of Jenny Colon but also of his maternal grandfather and grandmother and of his aunt Eugénie. Their bodies, however, had been transferred to the Clos de Nerval in 1836 when he was in Brussels. For a long time he searched for Jenny's grave in vain and then, remembering that he had precise directions as to its situation, he hurried home to consult them. The paper on which they were written, together with Jenny's last letter to him, was kept in a box containing souvenirs of his travels. Scattering this collection, he took up the two papers and was on the point of returning to the cemetery when again he was seized with remorse. 'I am not worthy', he told himself, 'to kneel at the grave of a Christian; I must not add a further profanation to so many others.'

Bewildered and confused, he went to stay at an inn outside Paris to allow the tumult in his brain to subside. But these alternating accesses of hope and remorse continued in his dreams. At one moment Aurélia appeared to him with a gesture of forgiveness, at another 'It is too late!' he cried, and voices repeated around him 'She is lost!' On his return next day he burned the two papers. It was a sacrifice with which, he hoped, God might be contented. Increasingly the threat of a fresh mental collapse hung over him. It seemed to him that the interval since his first serious illness twelve years before had been allowed him for repentance but that he had not profited by it. He had continued to lead the irresponsible and dissipated existence for which he now continually, though quite groundlessly, blamed himself. All his past life appeared to him in a more and more unfavourable light. Yet he still retained philosophic prejudices against certain dogmas and practices of the Christian religion and could not bring himself to go to confession. He had to work out his salvation in his own way. His ideal, the figure of Aurélia, existed only in his spiritual dream-world, and proof of the reality of her existence could lie only in the conviction of survival after death. It was the struggle to attain this faith in immortality that caused him ceaseless anguish.

His dreams grew more confused and terrifying and combined with the morbid reflections of his solitary life by day to reduce him to such a state of depression that he was scarcely able to speak. He could not read and understand ten consecutive lines. The company of his friends afforded him no relief. His mind was so completely occupied with his own mystical problems and illusions that communication with others failed. More and more he shunned them. Only Georges Bell patiently attended him. Together they took long walks in the country round about Paris. In an effort to rouse Gérard out of his despondency, Bell was content to do all the talking, only occasionally eliciting a desultory remark from his abstracted companion.

The fresh air and exercise had some effect, and Bell's eloquence did eventually succeed in bringing Gérard to a more positive frame of mind. There was yet time, he decided, to lead a good life and to make reparation for all the supposed ill he had done. He began by going to apologize to one of his acquaintance for some trivial negligence, and the satisfaction of having made amends, even in so slight a matter, buoyed him up. He had found a new motive for living and he began to take an interest in the world again. But it was only a temporary respite. His secret preoccupations hindered his work, and he found it more and more difficult to fulfil his obligations, particularly since people, seeing that he had apparently recovered his old self, became more exacting. In these circumstances it was impossible not to disappoint some of them, and the task of making reparations for all his lapses grew out of all proportion.

In the midst of all these difficulties came the news of the death of one of his friends, the poet Charles Renaud. Going to his rooms, where he had conversed with him only a month before, Gérard arrived just as the coffin was being nailed down. 'What would happen', he thought, 'if I were suddenly to die like that?' and immediately he was plunged again into the depths of gloom.

On the following Sunday he went, as usual, to call on his father whom, unfortunately, he found in an ill humour. The servant, Gabrielle, was ill. Dr Labrunie had to fetch wood from the loft and tersely refused his son's help. Gérard left the house supperless and thoroughly demoralized. He made his way to Montmartre but found the cemetery closed, a coincidence that he regarded as a bad omen. Did not everything conspire to come between him and his Aurélia? He decided to call on Heine in order to repay a sum of money advanced on a translation which he had not completed. At the Clichy gate he came upon two men fighting and tried to separate them, but without success. A few moments later, in reproach, as it seemed to him, for his having lacked strength to stop the fight, St Christopher appeared to him in the form of a tall and sturdy labourer carrying on his shoulder a child in a purple dress, the infant Christ. From that moment he wandered on in a limbo between reality and hallucination. As it was too late now to visit his friend Heine, he retraced his steps. Meeting a priest in the Rue de la Victoire, he asked if he might make his confession. The priest told him that he did not belong to that parish, but that, if he wished to consult him next day at Notre Dame, he had only to ask for the Abbé Dubois. Alas! it was rather to the Maison Dubois that Gérard's steps were once again leading him.

In desperation he went to Notre Dame de Lorette and flung himself down at the foot of the altar, begging forgiveness for his faults, but an inner voice seemed to whisper to him, 'The Virgin is dead, and your prayers are useless.' Thus betrayed by his lack of faith, his one thought was to atone by an act of renunciation. Kneeling at the end of the chancel, he slipped from his finger a ring engraved with the words 'Allah! Mohammed! Ali!', symbol of his Arabic beliefs and of his recognition of himself as a Cainite in revolt against conformist religion. At once candles were lit in the choir and a service began which his disordered mind apprehended only in a confused and disjointed manner. The lights were extinguished, and he stumbled out to make his way down the Champs Elysées to the Place de la Concorde. Given up to despair, his only thought was to destroy himself. Several times he approached the Seine with this intention, but some powerful influence seemed to restrain him. All at once the stars in the sky were extinguished, just as the candles in the church had been. The end of the world was come. In his delirium he saw only a black sun in the empty sky and a red globe of blood above the Tuileries. On reaching the Louvre, a strange spectacle awaited him. 'Through the clouds, which were racing with the wind, I saw several moons pass over at great speed. I thought that the earth had left its orbit and that it was drifting in the firmament like a dismasted vessel, now approaching, now receding from the stars which alternately grew larger and smaller.' He remained for two or three hours watching this chaotic phenomenon. Then he went to the market where the country folk were bringing in their produce, and he wondered what they would do when they realized that eternal night had begun, and 'yet the dogs barked here and there and the cocks crowed.'

Tired out at last, he went home to bed and was surprised, on waking, to see the light again. But there was little comfort in that, for the sun was cold and watery, and he presumed that it merely retained sufficient light to illuminate the earth for a few days yet before it should utterly consume itself. Accordingly he went to Heine's house and announced to him that all was finished and that they must prepare to die. Heine called his wife, who asked Gérard, 'What is the matter with you?' 'I don't know,' he replied. 'I am lost.' A cab was sent for and he was taken to the Maison Dubois.

This was on 6 February, and he was to remain there under treatment until 27 March. That it was a repetition of his breakdown of the year before he was well aware, for shortly afterwards he wrote to Liszt, 'I have suffered from a nervous illness involving a long convalescence and resulting from overwork occasioned by a drama played at the Porte Saint Martin in the winter of 1851.' Yet, desperately worried as he was by this relapse, it was only natural that he should try to minimize its effects in his correspondence. So even in a letter dated 11 February and addressed to Victorien de Mars of the *Revue des Deux Mondes* he wrote, 'it is not a real illness but heaviness of spirit'. But he found it impossible to work, and in the same letter he confessed, 'I am getting nowhere. It is deplorable. Perhaps it is because I want to do things too well. For I scratch out almost everything as I write. I am getting on better but there is nothing worse than having to fight against ill-health.'

Although his expenses at the Maison Dubois were paid for by the Ministry of Public Instruction, he emerged towards the end of March utterly without resources and it was only on 13 April that, after a further application, this time by Buloz, the Ministry of State granted him a subsidy of two hundred and fifty francs.

Towards the end of May, though still worried and depressed, he was gradually recovering the urge and the ability to write. By 10 June he felt himself completely recovered. In gratitude he wrote to Stadler, 'At last I am in thoroughly good health, for until recently I still had the blue devils. I am a miserable dog not to be able to tell you how much I owe to you and to what extent you have saved me this year as last. . . . No creature could be more grateful to another, but all that will be accounted for to you elsewhere; to tell you of my gratitude is all that I can do.'

When the sun shone and the trees were in leaf he seemed to be infused with new life; it was the dark, damp winter days that he dreaded. Now in summer he resumed his wanderings in the country round Paris. He visited Rheims Cathedral, but chiefly the old nostalgia drew him back to the Valois. Only there, in the quiet solitude of the woods and lanes round about Mortefontaine, could he find real peace of mind. He was busily at work on *Sylvie*. For all its apparent ease and simplicity, the work cost him a great deal of trouble, and particularly the corrections. He would be satisfied with nothing less than perfection. He finally delivered the copy to Buloz towards the end of July, but even at proof stage he was still polishing and correcting.

Sylvie appeared on 15 August 1853, but his delight at its accomplishment was overshadowed by the strain of its composition. A few days after its publication he began to suffer from a persistent insomnia. He would spend whole nights wandering about Montmartre and would watch the sun rise over Paris from the hill.

Sometimes he visited the markets and had long conversations with the country folk and labourers. He frequented the old haunts, too, Baratte's, Paul Niquet's, Mother Saguet's, and a gloomy tavern, the Cabaret de la Canne, situated on the Boulevard Rochechouart, where were displayed a number of walking-sticks carved by the landlord, one of which in particular, with its handle of mandragora root representing Apollo writhing amid flames, had a peculiar fascination for him.

Such an existence was in itself disquieting to his friends, but there were also more particular instances of eccentric and extravagant behaviour. For example, on one occasion he presented a parrot to Méry and on another, a lobster to Jules Janin. Then there were his visits to Busquet on three successive mornings accompanied by a Great Dane and two poodles, one black and one white. Again, it has been recorded that the poet Hérédia, who spent part of his youth at Senlis, was walking one day with his tutor in the country when they met Gérard carrying a cock under his cloak and were gravely informed that he was going to sacrifice it to Æsculapius. Subsequent incidents gave evidence of a definite disequilibrium, as when at Buloz's house he stepped into the kitchen one day during the cook's absence to open all the taps and leave them running.

The climax came on 24 August. On that evening he had supper at a café on the boulevard with his cousin, the young doctor Evariste Labrunie. Gérard's father had communicated to this man his fears for his son after a visit during which Gérard had seemed to be in an alarming state of excitability. Suddenly Gérard began to throw his money in the air, gold and silver coins. Then he strode off to the market. There he got into an argument with a complete stranger and struck him in the face. Prey now to the wildest hallucinations, he imagined himself surrounded by the ghostly armies of the Bourguignons and the Armagnacs and violently attacked a porter whom he took for Jean de Bourgogne. After wandering past the Tuileries and along the quays and then to the Luxembourg, he went back to breakfast with one of his friends. From there he went to Saint Eustache to kneel before the altar of the Virgin. It was in this church that his mother had been married and in thinking of her he shed tears which relaxed the tension in his mind. Leaving the church, he bought a silver ring. Then he went to pay a visit to his father. Finding him out, he left a bunch of marguerites at the house and walked on to the Jardin des Plantes. There he stood for some time watching a hippopotamus in a pool. Finally he threw his hat at it and went to visit the palaeontological galleries. The sight of the monsters exhibited there put him in mind of the Flood, and when he emerged again into the gardens in a regular downpour of rain, he believed it to be the beginning of a second universal deluge. The neighbouring streets were already inundated. Running down the Rue Saint Victor, he threw down the ring he had just bought in the deepest place, hoping by this sacrifice to save the world from disaster. Almost at once the storm abated, and a ray of sunlight broke through.

Filled with new hope, he set off to keep an appointment with Georges Bell. He arrived at the house tired and drenched through. Having changed his clothes, he lay down on Bell's bed and slept. In a dream the goddess Isis appeared to him saying, 'I am the same person as Mary, the same as your mother, the same, too, as all the forms you have already loved. After each of your ordeals, I have thrown off one of the masks beneath which I veil my features, and soon you will see me as I am.' Waking a little later, he said to his friend, 'Let us go out.' As they crossed the Pont des Arts, he explained at length the transmigration of souls. He was in a state of unusual exhilaration, and he said, 'It seems to me that this evening I have within me the soul of Napoleon, who inspires me and commands me to perform great things.' His behaviour was so peculiar that crowds began to gather as he made his way by the Palais-Royal arcades to the Rue Saint Honoré. There he went into a tobacconist's to buy a cigar, and when he came out the crowd was so dense that his friends were forced to rescue him and carry him off to the Charité Hospital.

All the symptoms of his former mental illness had reappeared, but in a more pronounced form. During the night his delirium increased and he had to be restrained in a strait-jacket. Somehow before morning he managed to free himself. Believing himself imbued with god-like power, he walked about the wards placing his hands upon the sick and inveighing against the ignorance of the doctors who believed they could cure by science alone. To prove the impotence of their art, he seized a bottle of ether and drank it off at a draught. Then he strode barefooted into the garden where he began gathering flowers. A friend of his, the painter Chenavard, came to visit him, and while they were talking someone crept up behind and slipped the strait-jacket over his shoulders again. He was put into a cab and taken to Dr Blanche's sanatorium at Passy.

Finding himself cloistered among lunatics, he realized that all he had experienced had been mere illusion. This was, he believed, but one more of the ordeals that Isis had told him he was destined to undergo. But still the illusions continued. He imagined that all the people about him were engaged in determining anew the movements of the heavenly bodies. It was his belief 'that an error had crept into the general arrangement of numbers, and that thence arose all the misfortunes of mankind.' His role 'seemed to be to re-establish universal harmony by cabbalistic art and to seek a solution by evoking the occult powers of various religions.' The old doubts and self-recriminations alternated with moods of triumph in which he felt informed with an invincible power, when 'everything in nature acquired a new aspect, and secret voices issued from plant and tree, from animals and from the humblest insects, to warn and encourage me. The speech of my companions took new and mysterious turns, the meaning of which I understood; formless and inanimate objects lent themselves to my esoteric calculations; from combinations of stones, shapes of corners, cracks or openings, patternings of leaves, colours, scents and sounds, emerged harmonies till then unknown. "How", I asked myself, "have I been able to exist so long outside nature and without identifying myself with it?" '

It was on 26 August that he had been conveyed to the Charité hospital, and he was transferred to Passy on the 27th. On 1 September he wrote to his father, 'You know how pleased I was, last time I saw you, with a business that had just ended favourably for me.[1] My delight induced some nervous excitement, and I am at Passy, with friends, in a superb house in lovely gardens. Do not be uneasy about this place where I must spend a few days. It is merely a matter of my having to recover complete health.' It did, indeed, seem that he was well on the way to recovery but when towards the end of September he left Passy, it was only to suffer a severe relapse so that he had to be taken back by force and subsequently subjected to a much more rigorous regimen. Only Stadler and Bell were allowed to visit him.

He had given up his room in the Rue du Mail and the few possessions he had amassed there had to be removed by 8 October. An old man now, harassed by his own worries (his faithful servant Gabrielle had died recently), Dr Labrunie was scarcely in a position to attend to his son's affairs. At the same time his inflexibility towards him had not relaxed. It must have seemed to him that his son, by his chosen way of life, had brought disaster upon himself. On this occasion in reply to an enquiry from Dr Blanche he wrote, 'I have sent to the Rue du Mail; Gérard's room is let. I cannot receive his effects at my house; my apartment is too small; I have only my servant's little room, but it is filled

---

[1] The publication of *Sylvie*.

with her things, which her heirs, whom I do not know, are not ready to remove. Gérard can say more or less what he wants done in the matter. No doubt one of his friends might be of use to him. As for me, who am alone and barely get along, I cannot even supply any information and I cannot be of use to him in any way.'

For his part Gérard was full of consideration for his father. On 7 October he wrote to him :

I thought I had done with this strange nervous excitement, but it overtook me again a week ago. Today I am very well. . . . I am told that you were informed, but I am afraid they may have mentioned the removal of my things which must be effected tomorrow, 8 October, before midday. One cannot concern oneself with such matters at your age, even if it were for oneself. Do not pay any money; I have the wherewithal to meet this expense, if my friends are not out of Paris, or if I am allowed to go and collect the money that I am owed.

I do not know how Gabrielle is; you see I was unable to do anything for her, that is another worry that I have involuntarily caused you, but I do believe that there is nothing to be really concerned about and that all will go well with her.[1] Above all do not part with any money, for I would not trust any who might ask it of you, having been brought here in singular circumstances and by people whom I suspect. As for my nervous excitement, I cannot deny it, but who is the cause of it? *Videbimus infra.* Do not give the order for the removal of my effects, for I have papers that I should not wish to see in just anybody's hands; we are living in a time of conspiracies and I distrust everyone, except those whom I feel to be friendly. There are few of them.

He had no real reason to suspect the people who had brought him back to Passy, for one of the two was Bernard Lopez, who had collaborated with him in *Les Montenegrins.* Once again Gérard was troubled by ideas of persecution. There were even occasions when he regarded Dr Blanche in an unfriendly light and one day he lay in wait for him in the garden, hiding behind a tree, and hurled a great stone at him which fortunately missed its mark. Clearly he was in no state to be released to attend to his own affairs, and it was Georges Bell who finally took charge of the removal of his belongings, Dr Blanche having decided that, since his patient would evidently require prolonged treatment, it would be best to bring his things to Passy to furnish his room there.

---

[1] Evidently he had not been informed of her death.

Gérard was delighted to have them about him again. With loving care he arranged the heterogeneous collection of relics, ranging over forty years of his life. There was an arrow kept in memory of archery meetings in Valois during his youth; there were pictures and pieces of furniture rescued from the demolition of the Rue du Doyenné; there were odd articles brought back from his eastern travels; and there were also, of course, his books, 'a queer collection of the knowledge of all periods, history, travel, religion, the Cabbala, astrology, which would have rejoiced the shades of Pico de la Mirandola, the sage Meursius and Nicholas de Cusa – the tower of Babel in two hundred volumes – all that had been left me! There was enough to make a fool of a wise man; not to say enough also to make a wise man of a fool.' It pleased him to think that it was 'a room cluttered with oddments like that of Dr Faustus'. And in this room at the end of a corridor, with a window overlooking the trees in the garden, he spent hours sorting out his papers, notes, and correspondence.

At Dr Blanche's suggestion he had begun to write an account of his illness. Doubtless it was intended not only as an innocuous occupation but also as a form of therapy in which by endeavouring to give a detailed objective account of them he might finally rid himself of his hallucinations. For a time he enjoyed some tranquillity of mind and, his thoughts turning again to Mortefontaine, he entered into negotiations with his aunt Labrunie for the purchase by annuity of her portion of the Clos de Nerval. He would not wish strangers to own the land in which his maternal relatives were buried, he explained, but at the same time it was his secret ambition to reconstitute the whole property which had been split up among several heirs. This had long been a major obsession with him and it was extended, during one of his periods of more extreme mental aberration, to include the project of marrying the Baroness Adrien de Feuchères (who had long since been dead) and so acquiring the whole domain of Mortefontaine. Maxime du Camp, calling to see him one day, was greeted by Gérard with this extraordinary pronouncement: 'It is kind of you to come and visit me; this poor Blanche is mad; he believes he is in charge of an asylum and we pretend to be deranged to humour him; you will take my place, for tomorrow I have to go to Chantilly to marry Mme de Feuchères.'

Despite short periods of better health, his depression deepened again towards the end of November on the anniversary of his mother's death. On the 27th he wrote to Georges Bell, 'I have much work to do to put my affairs in order. Winter is coming on and courage fails me, seeing that I have so little time and so little liberty at my disposal.' In the more lucid intervals of his illness it was the lack of liberty that most irked him. 'My ambition', he wrote, 'has always been only to see everybody happy around me, if I could deserve to be happy in my turn! I am charmed by the tranquillity one enjoys in his house and it fills me with kindly feelings. It would be paradise if I could enjoy a little liberty.' In a moving letter to Dr Blanche he begged to be allowed to visit his father :

Dare I ask you to allow me to go tomorrow, Sunday to see my father? This poor old man, in whom you have taken an interest, must be very sad; the sight of me and the certainty that I am well on the way to recovery will beyond doubt be a comfort to him. One grows old quickly at his age and, at mine, time passes also. By the tears I sincerely shed for your father,[1] I implore you to grant me this satisfaction. Do not imagine that I put the pleasure of seeing my friends above such a sacred duty. I can resign myself to receiving visits rarely, but the sight of my father would restore my moral strength and would give me energy to continue my work which, I believe, cannot but be useful and honourable for your establishment. In this way I succeed in ridding my head of all the visions which have so long occupied it. These unhealthy phantasmagoria will be succeeded by wholesome ideas, and I shall be able to appear in the world again as a living proof of your care and your talent. It is above all a moral cure that you will have effected for me and you will have re-established in society a writer who can still render some service. It is a friend first and foremost and an admirer that you have won.

Dr Blanche could not resist such an appeal. He sent for Evariste Labrunie to accompany Gérard to his father's house.

The visit refreshed him, and he returned to work with renewed vigour. He had begun *Aurélia* in a mood of eager optimism. The mere fact that he was writing again gave him confidence. He had told his father, 'I have undertaken to write and record all the impressions left by my illness. It will be a study of some use for observation and science. I have never had greater facility of analysis and description.' But by the end of the month he was already complaining to Georges Bell, 'What I am writing now revolves too much in a restricted circle. I feed on my own substance and do not renew myself.'

At the same time he was occupied in preparing the *Filles du Feu* for publication in the spring and he had also begun work on a

---

[1] Dr Esprit Blanche had died in the previous year.

novel, *L'Illustre Brisacier,* which was to have appeared in the *Mousquetaire.* But although the fact that Dumas had paid him an advance of sixty francs on this project served to keep it in his mind for some time, it never advanced beyond the first pages, which he printed in the introduction to the *Filles du Feu* addressed to Dumas.

On 10 December there appeared in the *Mousquetaire* an article by Dumas introducing the sonnet 'El Desdichado', and also announcing the production of Gérard's translation of Kotzebue's *Misanthropy and Repentance,* although, as it turned out, this piece was not actually produced until after his death in 1855. Gérard, who had every reason to conceal as far as possible his recent mental aberrations, was not altogether pleased with the article. Nevertheless, for the time being, he contented himself with protesting mildly that it was 'a little eccentric'. Later, replying to it in the dedicatory introduction to the *Filles du Feu,* he endeavoured to give a logical explanation of his 'supposed' madness.

The fact was that Dumas, like many others of his friends, had accustomed himself to regarding Gérard as out of his mind and no longer to be taken very seriously. In the article he had written : 'His is a charming and distinguished mind, as you may have judged, in which, from time to time, there occurs a certain phenomenon which, fortunately, we hope, is not greatly disturbing either for himself or for his friends; from time to time, when some work has intensely absorbed him, imagination, that madman in the house, momentarily drives out reason, which is only its mistress; then the former reigns alone, omnipotent, in this brain nourished on dreams and hallucinations.'

The hallucinations continued intermittently. Aurélia, in her numerous transformations, was his one guiding star. Courageously he faced his ordeal, seeking the faith that should restore to him in another life the woman whom he still loved, so that he need no longer hear only 'the voice of a dream, but the sacred promise of God'. There were times when the most terrible dreams and visions pursued one another in his disordered mind. But 'once persuaded that I was writing my own history, I set myself to translate all my dreams, all my emotions, I was tender towards this love for a fugitive *star* which abandoned me, alone in the night of my destiny and I wept, I trembled before the vain apparitions of my sleep. Then a divine ray shone into my hell; surrounded by monsters against whom I fought in obscurity, I seized the thread of Ariadne, and from that moment all my visions became divinely beautiful.'

It was after a particularly violent attack, during which he

shouted and sang and had to be locked into a cell where he suffered the most terrifying visions, that Dr Blanche succeeded in interesting him in the case of a young man, also in the asylum, formerly a soldier in Africa, who had refused food for six weeks and lay as if dead, never even opening his eyes. Gérard was filled with compassion for the young man. He would sit for hours bending over him and holding his hands. It seemed to him that, lying there between life and death, by a kind of hypnotic communication between their spirits, the youth offered direct access to the ear of God. At last one day he uttered a word. Gérard was overcome with joy. It was his own will, he believed, that had evoked the first sign of recovery.

That night he had a delightful dream.

I was in a tower, reaching so deep into the earth and so high towards the sky, that it seemed my whole life would have to be spent in climbing up and down. Already my strength was failing, and I was just losing courage when a door in the side opened; a spirit appeared to me and said : 'Come, brother!' I do not know why, but I had the idea that he was called Saturnin. He had the features of the poor sick man, but transfigured and actively intelligent. We were in a countryside which lay open to the stars; we stopped to survey the scene, and the spirit stretched out his hand over my forehead as I had done the day before in an attempt to hypnotize my companion; immediately one of the stars I was looking at in the sky began to grow larger and the divinity of my dreams appeared to me smiling, in an almost Indian costume, just as I had seen her of old. She walked along between us, and the meadows grew green, flowers and foliage sprang up from the earth in the track of her footsteps. . . . She said to me : 'The ordeal to which you have been submitted has come to its end; those countless stairs that you tired yourself going up and down were the same bonds of old illusions which hampered your thoughts, and now recall the day when you supplicated the Holy Virgin and when, believing her dead, you were seized with delirium. Your prayer had to be carried to her by a simple soul disengaged from earthly ties. She is near you, and that is why I am permitted to come and encourage you.'

From this time, he says, 'I resolved to fix my dreams in my mind and learn the secret of their meaning. "Why not", I asked myself, "at last force these mystic gates, armed with all my will, and dominate my sensations instead of submitting to them? Is it not possible to subdue this fascinating and fearful chimera, to impose a rule on these night spirits which play with our reason?" '

Gradually the young man, so jealously watched by Gérard, began to recover. He opened his eyes and began to talk intermittently, but still he had to be fed forcibly. When Gérard asked why he would not eat, he replied that he was dead and had been buried, and that now he was in purgatory fulfilling his expiation. The recognition of the close parallel with his own case enabled Gérard finally to emerge from the realm of illusion which had so long claimed him. As had been foretold in his dream, his own ordeal was over, his expiation accomplished.

His one anxiety now was to conceal the gravity of his illness and resume his former life as if without interruption. In the *Mousquetaire* of 6 May 1854, Philibert Audebrand had written of him, 'He is a charming poet, whom everybody loves and who, it is said, must spend the summer in Cairo, where Méry will follow him; . . . one would be very happy to see him leave for the Orient which he loves almost as much as Germany; but at the same time one would be sorry at his going away. But where is he? Where is Gérard de Nerval? Georges Bell claims to have seen a letter announcing his arrival at Malta. A few hours and he will be in Egypt. If this is true, and if this new long voyage he has undertaken is already begun, may God guide him and a protecting fairy always lead him by the hand!'

'Alas!' wrote Gérard to Georges Bell, 'I am not at Malta but at Passy where I have been ill and very sad these last few days. M. Blanche undertook to warn my friends and I believe you were told of my sad story. Try to prevent people from talking about it, since my indisposition, which happily is not a relapse, has already been misfortune enough for me.'

Shortly afterwards, on 27 May, he left the clinic at Passy, apparently cured and free once more to follow his own fancy.

14

The Last Journey

Freedom for Gérard, meant freedom to travel, but this time, too, he was eager to escape from Paris where the spectre of his illness awaited him everywhere in the sympathy of his friends and acquaintances, as he well knew after the bitter experience of his first illness. Then, on his recovery, in reference to Janin's article of 1 March 1841, he had written, 'It is three months, my dear Janin, since you were pleased to celebrate the good fortune and the *leisure* which I owe to the State, flinging your *night-cap* to me over the windmills of Montmartre, which ought to help, you said, to preserve the happy innocence in which I live. Since that time, those of my friends who do not believe me dead, and there are some who persist in not *recognizing* me, continue to lament my lost *reason*, and approach me with expressions of condolence, . . . so that, my dear Janin, I am the living tomb of the Gérard de Nerval whom you have loved, published and encouraged for so long.' He could not face the prospect of repeating such an experience. As he had written in the *Voyage en Orient,* he was 'ashamed of suffering, like the animal that retires into solitude to suffer long or to die there without complaint.'

Early in March Francis Wey had addressed a letter to the Minister of Public Instruction on behalf of the Society of Men of Letters, in which he wrote :

Owing to your Excellency's generous solicitude, one of the most brilliant writers in our society, Mr Gérard de Nerval, who was lately overtaken by a serious illness, has been the object of diligent care resulting in a complete recovery. Your kindness has restored his life; a new favour would restore to literature and to the public our colleague's distinguished talent. In the opinion of the doctors, Gérard will only recover the full faculty of his mind if he travels. But impoverished as the result of a long forced rest, he is not in a position to set out on his own resources alone. . . .

In granting our colleague a sum of 600 francs which he

cannot do without, your Excellency would be encouraging a man of recognized merit, in all probability endowing literature with a good book, and bestowing benefactions in a profitable manner.

The appeal had been successful, and on 14 March 1854 Gérard had been informed by the minister that he was entrusted with a mission to the Orient for the purpose of continuing his literary work. He was granted a subsidy of six hundred francs on the understanding that he would send frequent reports to the minister on his researches and observations.

Dr Blanche, who was by no means completely assured of his patient's recovery, although he could no longer detain him against his will, viewed the proposed journey with alarm. He could not approve of an undertaking which would expose Gérard to hardships and excitements likely to aggravate his condition. His friendship, his care and his interest in Gérard had fully won the poet's confidence, and his opinion and advice carried great weight with him. Under his influence Gérard abandoned the larger project for the time being and decided to confine his travels to Germany. Accordingly, after a hurried settlement of his most pressing affairs in Paris, he left for Strasbourg on 27 May, the same day on which he was released from Passy. Besides the six hundred francs from the ministry he had fifteen hundred francs advanced by the Comédie-Française for *Misanthropy and Repentance,* but there were some debts which he cleared with his customary scrupulousness at the earliest opportunity.

Germany had for so long now seemed like a second home to him that as soon as he had crossed the border he was inspired with new confidence. In a letter to his father he wrote, 'My works are a capital which I shall increase, please God, and which, even if only after death, will be sufficient to acquit me in men's eyes. . . . Travel, movement, solitude even, for I have too many acquaintances and distractions in Paris, have restored my moral strength and, I believe also, my talent. . . . If I have debts, I have time to pay them and it is known that I do what I can.'

He was still engaged on *Aurélia* for the *Revue de Paris,* and he was revolving other projects in his head, the completion of his novel, *Brisacier,* and a piece for the theatre, *La Belle Gabrielle,* in which he was to collaborate with Maquet but which eventually Maquet completed alone. He seemed to have experienced a spiritual renewal. On returning to Strasbourg after an excursion to Baden, he wrote enthusiastically to Georges Bell, 'Wonderful! On reaching the banks of the Rhine I have found my voice again and my *powers*!' Always the crossing of the Rhine had, for him, a magical effect. In bringing him back to the country where his mother was buried, it was analogous to a crossing of the Styx into the limbo of departed spirits where he might feel somehow in closer communication with her who continually haunted his dreams. Recalling the vicissitudes of his visit to Strasbourg in 1838, he told Bell, 'I am not staying at the Raven any more – that was too sinister,[1] but I feel myself already blazing like a star, and, for some time extinguished, I am rekindled at the old *Sun* of my best days.'

However he could not altogether suppress his regrets and anxieties, regrets for not having bid goodbye to all his friends before leaving Paris, particularly Dumas to whose daughter he sent a sprig of forget-me-not gathered 'at the foot of the slippery rocks where the Lorelei appeared'; anxieties still to make reparation for his faults, and he begged his friend to search out the man he had struck in the Paris market in his delirium of the previous summer and to make his apologies, promising at the same time to compensate him.

In the same letter he speaks of the portrait, engraved by E. Gervais, that had just appeared in Mirecourt's biographical brochure. It had been lent to him by Charles Mehl, a book-lover of Strasbourg, and he had returned the copy marked with various cabbalistic signs and the inscription 'I am the other' beneath the portrait. 'The artist', Gérard says, 'is a talented man, more serious than Nadar, whose pencil is tipped only with wit;[2] but like our red-haired friend, he is *too faithful*. Tell everyone that it is a good likeness but posthumous – or rather that Mercury has assumed the features of Sosie[3] and posed in my place. I will wash my face with ambrosia, if the gods allow me only half a glass.'

In this portrait he recognized his favoured double. The face, with its clear eyes and firm, smooth cheeks, is placid and self-assured; the delicate hand is posed artificially against the chin, not

---

[1] It is evident that here Gérard has in mind Poe's 'Raven', with which he was deeply impressed. There was too close an analogy between Poe's 'sainted maiden', the 'Lost Lenore', and his own Aurélia, 'for ever lost', for the poem not to have struck him forcefully as a painful reminder of his own situation, and we may even recognize an echo of the raven's baleful refrain of 'nevermore' in the insistent repetition of 'too late' in *Aurélia*.

There can be little doubt that even at this time Gérard was acquainted with the raven that haunted the steps of the lodging-house in the Rue de la Vieille Lanterne. This, too, was a bird of ill omen, and it is perhaps not too fanciful to suppose that, in those sordid surroundings, it may have seemed so to him, though he would scarcely then have known why.

[2] The reference is to a caricature by Nadar.

[3] See note, p 109.

supporting it. This, certainly, is not the real Gérard, whose deep-set, penetrating eyes gaze directly out above the sunken cheeks of Nadar's photograph, seeming to see through and beyond the object of their vision. Here is the lined face of a man who has suffered, humble and sympathetic; the hands in his lap are restless even in repose. There is little here to recall the gaiety and lightness, the elegance of his youth. Essentially the features are the same, the oval face, the high forehead, large nose and rounded chin, the clear complexion, the grey eyes, and chestnut hair and beard, but it is in the expression that one may recognize something of Houssaye's description of him: 'Gérard was charming, with the softness of a dove, the lightness of a cloud. One was immediately captured by his eyes which were his soul, by his voice which was his heart. There was something slightly feminine in the Napoleonic face.' That Gérard was conscious of having aged considerably has already been remarked. 'Illness', he said, 'has made me so ugly – melancholy so neglectful.' He no longer cared much about his appearance, and was often ragged and upkempt.

A month later, having read Mirecourt's biographical brochure, he pronounced it 'exaggerated and full of errors, but fundamentally true, if there is not too much raillery in the absolute eulogy of me he presents, always at the expense of others.' He was afraid that it might make him enemies, and he was a trifle piqued by the suggestion that he had paid eight thousand francs for the famous bed in the Rue du Doyenné. He regretted not having read the account in proof, but he was struck by the truths contained in it and accepted it with humility. 'One cannot prevent people from talking,' he wrote to his father; 'it is in this way that history is written, which proves that I have done well to keep my poetic life separate from my real life.'

Before Gérard left Passy Dr Blanche had urged him to write to him frequently during his travels, informing him of his progress. Gérard, eager to assure the doctor of his recovery, wrote regularly, giving a detailed account of his journey and of his condition. In his first letter, addressed from Baden on 1 June, he showed himself full of hope and good intentions. 'My mind', he wrote, 'is so well ordered that at last I foresee I shall be able to produce some good work for the winter and some good descriptive letters; I should be very much to blame if I did not turn your kindness and the care of my friends to the profit of literature and art.' He begged Blanche to explain to his former companions at Passy 'that the pensive being they saw creeping about, uneasy and morose in the sitting-room, in the garden or beside your hospitable table, was assuredly not I. From the other side of the

Rhine, I disown the sycophant who took my name and perhaps my face.'

Throughout the letters written at this period his gratitude to Dr Blanche and to his friends is constantly evident; to Blanche who had been 'doctor to me above all morally and that is what I needed' and whose 'house is an enchanted palace that is not easy to leave'; to Anthony Deschamps, translator of the *Divina Commedia* and for a long time a patient at Passy, with whom he had formed a close friendship, 'for all his good advice and his always so lively conversation which raised my spirits and gave me up to the last moment ideas from which I hope to profit now'; to Francis Wey for 'the trouble you have taken for me just as Eugène [de Stadler] has; but I shall not forget that I have found your helping hand to the end.'

In accordance with Dr Blanche's wishes Gérard had decided to avoid distractions and excitement as much as possible. For this reason he had brought no letters of introduction with him, and settled down quietly at the Hotel de la Fleur.

But that he was far from cured was very evident, even to himself. Despite the strict regimen recommended by Blanche, which he was careful to observe, his fits of elation and depression continued to succeed each other as before, and the least irregularity was liable to upset his equilibrium. On 4 June, only five days after his arrival in Strasbourg, he wrote to his father, 'There was every reason to advise discretion. The disorder, that is to say the exaltation, has returned at times, or rather at certain times. I must pass here for a prophet (a false prophet), with my sometimes mystical language and my frequent abstraction. I am, like you, short-sighted; I greet someone, and he does not reply; I do not reply when someone greets me, one is the cause of the other, and sometimes I fancy people are seriously annoyed. I end by accustoming myself without a qualm to never being polite to more than one in five. In fact, like father like son; you, too, have made many enemies owing to short sight and not to negligence.'

His sociable nature demanded company but in general he avoided large gatherings, knowing his tendency to become over-excited after taking a few drinks. One evening, having made friends with a company of students at a ball and drunk too much beer, he made so much noise in the Hotel de la Fleur, where he was staying, that some of the guests left. The incident was passed over quietly, but it inevitably increased his anxiety and although he related it in detail to his friend Sartorius, to Blanche he merely confessed to 'a slight relaxation of the regimen on one occasion'. He had reason to be concerned, for this was no mere drunken orgy but a return of his mental disorder. Certainly drink had the effect of exacerbating his condition, but it was not the cause of it. Consequently, when later at Weimar he again met Liszt, who was about to leave for Rotterdam and tried to persuade him to go with him, he reluctantly refused. 'My health', he wrote on this occasion, 'cannot stand numerous company; and, whilst calm during my solitary wanderings, I have to beware of rapid conversation, discussions, and the attraction of dinners and suppers.'

He had left Strasbourg on 5 June without any fixed plan. His itinerary varied a good deal, 'according to the facilities of the railway or the boat and also according to the weather', as he wrote from Stuttgart after a five-day visit to Karlsruhe; 'this is a journey so devoid of adventures and risks that I see in it only one end, distraction, the need to rid myself of black thoughts and to throw off the last clouds.' The clouds, however, were not so easily dispersed. The mood of despondency persisted. During the course of his subsequent peregrinations, which took him on a circular journey by way of Bruschal, Stuttgart, Munich, Augsburg, Donauwörth, Nuremberg, Bamburg, Neuenmarkt, Leipzig, Weimar, Cassel and Frankfurt, to Forbach, there were moments of optimism, as when he wrote to Georges Bell, 'My mind is cleared and I have regained the robust health of younger days. I have discovered new abilities in myself.' But he was continually beset by anxieties. Under the constant threat of a return of his mental illness, his great fear was that his creative faculties might fail him, for he had not written as much as he had expected to during these weeks in Germany.

A further source of anxiety was the lack of news of his father. Now more than ever, in his solitary wanderings, he was conscious of the distance between them, and blamed himself for this estrangement. 'Do not imagine,' he wrote on 20 June, 'when I am far away, that I am not near you all the same. I shall be near you still, even in the tomb. If I should die before you, perhaps at the last moment the thought would occur to me that you have never really known me. But that will come . . . the older I grow the more of you I feel in me.' Such sentiments were dictated as much by his loneliness as by his genuine feeling for his father. The incompatibility of their temperaments remained an insurmountable obstacle between them.

Gérard wrote to his father regularly from Germany, constantly assuring him of his recovery, detailing the course of his journey, describing the places he had visited, and recalling to the old man his younger days with the army, as when from Leipzig he wrote, 'I have met here a worthy man of just about your age, also an old soldier, who gave me very interesting details about the battle of Leipzig. He showed me the place where Poniatowsky perished in the Elster. The river is small, but so swift that one can well understand the misfortunes it caused. Twelve thousand Frenchmen met their death there or were thrown into it; I listened with tears in my eyes to all the details of these disasters. This worthy man is a hotel-keeper with whom I lunched and passed half a day talking of France and of those times. I told him your story and he kept saying "Is it possible?", taking great interest in a man of the same age as himself happily well preserved like him.' These letters evoked no reply, and Gérard's consequent anxiety about his father increased his sense of guilt and remorse. 'It is not the future that worries me,' he wrote to him, 'but the sad feeling of all that relates to the past. I would wish you to be quite easy about me, but I always reproach myself bitterly for the reasons I have so many times given you for anxiety.'

It was Gérard's intention, on leaving Leipzig, to attend the musical festivals at Eisenach in honour of Wagner but, because of bad weather, these did not take place. A few days later he went on to Weimar to stay with Liszt until the latter left for Rotterdam, but where he went during the interim is not known. In view of the subsequent intensification of his obsessions and anxieties, it has been very plausibly suggested by M. Jean Richer that he may have gone to visit his mother's grave at Glogau and that this brought about the final relapse. Such a pilgrimage would have been the logical climax of his last visit to Germany, and indeed of his whole life's journey, for the figure of his lost mother had not ceased to haunt his imagination in dream and vision throughout the years. Certainly, too, there were signs of grave mental disturbance at this time for, writing to Liszt in the following autumn, he begged to be excused for certain oddities of behaviour during his two-day visit to Weimar which must have seemed inexplicable to the composer at the time. There can be little doubt, moreover, that, if he did actually undertake the journey he had so often made before in spirit, it must have revived very forcibly all his old resentment against his father as the one responsible for his mother's death and this, in conflict with his earnest desire for reconciliation, must have excited still further self-recriminations, fresh thoughts of repentance and expiation.

Writing to Dr Blanche from Cassel on 11 July to express his pleasure at the news of the doctor's forthcoming wedding, he tells how at Leipzig he had seen a lovely young child and, on asking its name, had been told that it was Emile. This, he says, must be taken for a good omen, at the same time excusing himself for still being subject to superstitious ideas. He goes on to speak of his father, and it is here that the agony of mind induced by the familiar obsessions and his utter dependence on Blanche became painfully apparent. 'I have not received any news of him and for some days I have suffered a great deal thinking of him. Blanche, whatever you think of me, for there are many hard things in your letters, send to him quickly. Write to me poste restante at Frankfurt. I am in tears as I write this to you, and, if that is not a sign of regret, how should I know whether I have been right or wrong, whether I am good or bad? Write to me, my heart swells when I think of you, when I think of him. Write and tell me what I must do, for I am really suffering and in my heart. If there is always a moment for repentance, well! I repent, but I am still walking in darkness, and it is your reply and your advice that I am waiting for.'

It was a desperate cry. 'Am I good or bad? Am I the good or the evil genius?' He still could not resolve the problem of his dual nature. It was essential for his purpose of winning Aurélia that he should be 'the good'. The ordeal of his first mental illness had in his view been a warning, but he had disregarded it. Ten years had been allowed him in which to repent and he had not profited by them at all. Recalling Molière's *Don Juan,* he wrote in *Aurélia,* 'After the visit of *the stone guest,* I had sat down again at the feast!' After his second 'descent into Hell' he had emerged triumphant, assured of his Eurydice. But now under the threat of a third such ordeal his confidence wavered. He could no longer be sure of himself. Again he heard the voices that had echoed in his delirium crying 'She is lost.' Perhaps after all it was 'Too late'. 'Scripture', he wrote in a series of notes that were published after his death, 'says that in order to be saved repentance is sufficient, but it must be sincere. And if the event that strikes you prevents this repentance? If you are thrust into a state of fever, of madness? If the gates of redemption are closed to you? . . .'

The shadows were again closing in upon him. On 15 July he wrote to Dr Blanche from Frankfurt, 'The sickness is greater than you think; however I have done nothing with which anyone can reproach me and I have wronged only myself. . . . Perhaps any oddity in my behaviour exists only for me, whose brain is abundantly nourished with visions and who have trouble to separate real life from the life of dream. . . . What I am conscious of above all is your extreme kindness and your sympathy for a poor sick man who has done everything to avoid your advice. . . . peace in myself, I still hope to find it again. . . . my chief worry in all my moments of solitude has always been the thought of my father. Do not imagine that I tell you this again in order to gain your sympathy, but the hurt I have caused him to suffer continually weighs on my heart. If I were destined to offer an example of the most grievous expiation that one can imagine, I should submit to it willingly at the thought of this alone.'

Four days later, on reaching France, he had recovered some measure of equanimity. From Bar le Duc he wrote to Dr Blanche, 'I was wrong, no doubt, not to have had more confidence; but anxiety caused me terrible days and nights; I am reassured as I draw nearer to you and to our friends; what is the good of doubt and despair?' and to his father 'I am returning after having made a long tour. . . . I hope you will not be alarmed by some excitability which has moderated more and more; nor by a certain sadness I have felt lately. An illness such as I have so long been subject to always leaves some traces and the first days of liberty are a probation. All things considered, I believe I have at last surmounted it. . . . At my age I really feel I am no longer fit for extended travels. . . . Blanche's last letter has reassured me. He is an excellent man whom I get to know better every day. . . . I am going to set to work on my return. . . . The main thing is not to lose confidence for anxiety leads to nothing.'

Hope seems to have revived in him. On arriving in Paris on 20 July, his first thought was to report to the Society of Men of Letters, giving a full account of the results of his mission concerning translation rights abroad. The first part of *Aurélia* was already in the press, and he was engaged in arranging to secure the copyright of the book in England and in Spain. At the same time he entered into negotiations for an edition of his complete works.

All these simultaneous activities and anxieties now proved too much for him. The mental derangement that had threatened him again and again during his travels in Germany now manifested itself in a more acute form and on 6 August 1854 he was taken back to Passy in a deplorable state of uncontrolled delirium.

15

Face to Face

Gérard's hopes of a complete and permanent recovery were dwindling. Previously he had submitted without protest to Dr Blanche's treatment, but now he could no longer believe that it had any real effect on his condition. Revolting against what seemed to him a purely arbitrary curtailment of his liberty, he grew so violent that he had to be forcibly restrained.

Within a week of his arrival at Passy he made his escape and appeared one evening at Busquet's apartment in a pitiful state. 'Ah! It's horrible,' he complained to his friend, 'they have made me suffer too much! Look at my wrists, they are bruised; look at my feet: my ankles are stiff and swollen. If only Blanche knew! They have tortured me! I have run away.' Tears streamed down his pallid face. His clothes were torn. Busquet took him in and tried to comfort him. For a while Gérard leaned on the window-sill, gazing at the ground below. Then, turning to his friend, he said, 'I was thinking that it would be a quick death to fall down there from your sixth floor! The idea of throwing myself from your window has occurred to me on several occasions.' Seriously alarmed, from that time on Busquet took good care that Gérard should never be allowed to go up to his rooms alone unless he was there.

For the next two weeks, fearful of being taken back to Blanche's, he avoided all contact with his friends. Apart from the fact that, according to Maxime du Camp, he spent two days at Creil where he stayed at a humble tavern frequented by labourers, nothing is known of his movements during that period, but at the end of it he returned to Passy of his own accord. Calmer now in mind, he submitted voluntarily to the closer supervision inevitably resulting from his truancy. Under Dr Blanche's care his condition steadily improved and by 21 September he was able to receive a visit from his cousin Evariste and his aunt Labrunie.

But with the gradual return of health and reason his anxieties about his work increased and together with them his restlessness. He was impatient to be free to attend to his affairs and fulfil his commitments. Again he felt that the care that was being taken for his health was hindering his work and jeopardizing his chances of avoiding further debts. On 23 September he wrote to Godefroy, the director and legal representative of the Society of Men of Letters, begging him to exert his influence to obtain some relaxation of Dr Blanche's strict vigilance. The result of his carefully worded and logically reasoned plea was the following demand addressed to the doctor on 9 October: 'We, the undersigned, friends of M. Gérard de Nerval, man of letters, beg leave to request Dr Blanche to agree to authorize M. Gérard de Nerval's departure, and the removal of all his effects, in accordance with the regulations obtaining in the establishment of which he is director and proprietor. Paris, 9 October 1854. Godefroy, Advocate.' To this was appended a note, 'Dear Sir, Gérard wishes me to sign this paper, and, as I have no reason to refuse him, I sign, trusting to what is easiest to do. With my compliments. J. Janin.'

Dr Blanche was taken completely by surprise. Gérard he knew, was in no fit state to be set at liberty, more particularly at the beginning of winter. Nevertheless, despite his fears for his patient and his resentment at this peremptory demand, possibly, too, at Gérard's seeming ingratitude, he had no alternative but to comply.

'My dear colleague,' he wrote to Evariste Labrunie on 11 October, 'your cousin, M. Gérard de Nerval is worrying me to give him his liberty. Knowing that he has no home in Paris, I cannot allow him to leave my house without first being sure that he has at least a room in which to put his things and where he can live. I apply to you first to know whether you intend to concern yourself with his affairs or whether, failing you, some member of your family will undertake to do so. I have, moreover, decided to entrust M. Gérard de Nerval to any of his relations or friends who will accept responsibility for the sick man in writing from the time he leaves my establishment. If neither relatives nor friends are willing to be burdened with him, I will advise the higher authority who will deal with the matter. You must know that at the time when M. Gérard de Nerval fell ill, M. Labrunie, his father, gave me to understand that he could not look after his son. With the respects, Sir and honoured colleague, of your very devoted servant, E. Blanche.'

Whilst thus ensuring his own freedom from further responsibility for Gérard, Dr Blanche was genuinely concerned for the welfare of the patient to whom he had given so much friendly care and sympathy, and his worst fears must have been confirmed on receipt of a letter from him dated 17 October, filled with masonic gibberish, which gives clear evidence of the unbalanced state of his mind. By then arrangements had already been completed for his leaving

Passy. His aunt Labrunie, who lived with her son Evariste in the Rue Rambuteau, undertook to receive him into her house until he should find suitable accommodation, asking only that his furniture and his few possessions might be left at Passy for a few days. In fact they remained there permanently and after his death were kept by Dr Blanche in memory of him, later to pass into the possession of his son, Jacques Emile Blanche.

Gérard left Dr Blanche's establishment on 19 October. Delighted with his new-found freedom, he wrote to Jules Janin, 'I have left with the honours of war but not with *arms and baggage*, as they say at St Pélagie. My furniture and books have been kept provisionally.' But although on the surface he seemed restored to normal and rational behaviour, the lurking insanity constantly emerged from the depths of his hallucinated mind, as in the following letter to Houssaye written the next day:

My poor dear Houssaye, I was not there when you called. Nevertheless you must have been very glad to find that I had left. Today I am going further, tomorrow most likely, I shall go to see Janin. Tell him what is requisite. There is no need to thank him – I am mad – I will bring him good luck and I will teach him to make gold. That is all. But it is so troublesome that he will not have enough patience, he will prefer to receive it ready-made from the good God – By the way there is one somewhere – in a cuckoo-clock – there are even several of them perhaps – I have been afraid of him. But you will think, my poor good friend, that I am still ill, as the Greeks[1] said! Janin fully understood – not everything – but he knows or will know everything.

Come and see me this evening if you can, or tomorrow morning.

He who was GERARD and who still is; γηρας, glory, honour recompense (to you all!)

Four days later he had already begun to regret his rebellious attitude towards Dr Blanche, and in a letter to Anthony Deschamps, referring to Passy, he wrote 'Everything is accomplished. Now I have only myself to blame and my impatience which has driven me out of *paradise*. Henceforth I work and bring forth in sorrow.'

Yet he still denied the serious nature of his illness: 'I agree officially that I have been ill. I cannot agree that I have been mad or even hallucinated.'

---

[1] At that time a slang term for rogues or cheats.

To his father he wrote on 2 November, 'I am very well and my former irritation is more and more allayed : Dr Blanche no longer seems as culpable towards me as he did at first. His friends have explained his conduct to me and what remains of my mistrust is only the result of natural resentment at having been so long deprived of my liberty.'

The thought of having forfeited Blanche's friendship preyed on his mind, affording an added stimulus to his sense of guilt. 'One important cause for complaint remains for me to define,' he wrote to Blanche himself on 7 November; 'it arises from finding myself rejected, as friend and guest, from the society of your relations and friends at Passy.'

Dr Blanche's reply, in which he shows himself to be a true and generous friend, reveals his grave concern for the patient who had deliberately rejected his help.

I am glad to hear that your prejudices on leaving as a sick man not yet cured are gradually disappearing. I look forward to the time when all your false ideas about the nature of the illness that attacked you and the care that you received will give place to true ones; for then you will be cured and you will find in the natural goodness of your heart the feelings of gratitude that you owe to your real friends, that is to say those who cared for you. As for me, without my friendship's having been altered by it, to my great regret I have had to renounce my attentions to you, which, since you did not receive them with confidence, would no longer be of use to you; at your repeated entreaties, I was obliged to send you back to your family and I was sorry to see you refuse a hospitality which I should have been happy to extend to you always.

When you left me, I told Mme Labrunie, your aunt, that you were not in a state to be left to your own devices, and that you would need constant superintendence; I have since been informed that my fears were only too well founded; at the same time I learned that you attributed the disturbed state of your mind to the mortification of not being able to pay me, and also to the thought that you would never again be received in a house in which you had lived for some time, and of which I had dreamed of your always being a guest. Not wishing to begin by deserving your reproaches, nor those of your friends, I hasten to reassure you. When you have no more prejudices against me, when you have a sane and sensible judgement of my conduct towards you and when in consequence you can take pleasure in seeing me, come; as for the money you owe me, since you call yourself my friend, treat me then as a friend and allow me to wait until your work shall have produced all that you hope, without giving me the anxiety of thinking that this preoccupation is preventing you from devoting yourself to it entirely.

In spite of such assurances to the contrary, Gérard continued to believe that Blanche was angered by the intractable attitude he had adopted. The fear of having permanently impaired their friendly relationship solely by his own fault tormented him. On 2 January 1855 he again wrote to him, expressing his remorse and excusing his impatience on the ground that it had been due only to the desire to continue his literary career. At the same time he apologized for not having removed his belongings; he had not yet found a suitable lodging.

Since he had left Passy he had had no permanent residence. He had rented a room at the Hotel de Normandie in the Rue Neuve des Bons Enfants, but he seldom slept there, nor at his aunt's. His vagrant nature had reasserted itself. As so often before, he spent whole nights wandering about Montmartre, the markets and the suburbs, sometimes mingling with sordid company in the cheapest all-night taverns frequented only by the poorest labourers, thieves, prostitutes and vagabonds. He slept little, and wherever occasion provided. During the day, too he wandered about the city in search of inspiration or sat in a café with the blank paper before him. He was still working on *Aurélia*, but his thoughts were confused and ideas came to him more and more fleetingly; he was scarcely writing twenty words a day.

Sometimes he visited his friends, Houssaye, Bell, Busquet, Stadler, Gautier, and even stayed for a day or two, but for the most part he led a solitary life, and no one knew where he spent his time. He had aged considerably. Though only forty-six years old, he might have passed for more than sixty. 'I have lost my taste for the wine of life,' he announced dispiritedly. He was no longer the gay companion of former times whose conversation had charmed and delighted his hearers. Instead he now talked mainly on strange and abstruse mystical matters which were quite beyond the comprehension of his friends or told them of his fantastic beliefs, such as that the treasure of the Medicis was buried under a tree in the Tuileries, or that the goldfish in the fountains swam to the surface to bring him messages from the Queen of Sheba.

Despite the strangeness of his conversation and behaviour his friends welcomed him cordially. As Théophile wrote, 'Which of us has not a dozen times prepared a room in the hope that Gérard would come to spend a few days there, for none dared hope that he might stay for a few months, so well-known was his free and errant humour! Like the swallow, when one leaves a window open, he came in, took two or three turns, found everything right and charming, and flew off to continue his dream in the street. This was not at all occasioned by heedlessness or coldness; but like the swift of the towers, which has no feet and whose life is a perpetual flight, he could not settle.'

More and more he was withdrawing from the world of reality into that of his dream. Even when he emerged for a while from the obscure region of his mystical visions his recollections were apt to be tinged with fantasy, although to a stranger he might appear to be perfectly normal and lucid, and something of the old charm still remained.

One evening Alfred Delvau was sitting at one of the three tables in the Cabaret de la Canne before a bottle of wine, with the house cat purring on his knees, when a man entered, shook the snow from his overcoat and sat down at the next table with a little glass. The newcomer leaned on his elbows, looked at Delvau, looked at the cat, drank off the little glass and shook his head, an intelligent head with a broad high forehead, bald and shining. Delvau returned his look. They exchanged a few casual words, and gradually warmed into conversation. Delvau listened, fascinated, as the stranger talked of the shady underworld of the city, of Montmartre where he said he had lived for some time, and of a Roman vine, the last from the vineyards celebrated since the time of the emperor Julian, which he had nearly bought, some years before, for the modest sum of three thousand francs and which was now worth thirty thousand. When they parted, at about two o'clock in the morning, although neither of them knew who the other was, they were the best of friends despite the difference in their ages.

Delvau was then publishing in a literary journal a series of studies of his contemporaries and when his first article on Gérard de Nerval appeared, he received a letter from him in which he wrote, 'What charming things you have said about my books. I dare not consider myself worthy of so much praise. But it comes to encourage me at a time when I need to lean on what I have done in order to try to do better, if my health still allows. I am happy to find myself supported by a writer who speaks authoritatively of style and who has such an exalted view of literary criticism.' The next day he happened to meet Gérard at a bookseller's and, learning his identity, was deeply mortified at not having recognized in the stranger of the Cabaret de la Canne the writer whom he so much admired.

Two days later the overcoat Gérard had worn on the occasion of his first meeting with Delvau was gone. It was not the first time that he had been forced to pawn his coat. In the course of his travels he had long before schooled himself to subsist on very little, but then, poor as he had often been, there had always been the prospect of a timely remittance arriving to save the situation. Now his meagre funds were exhausted, and he no longer had the power nor the will to supply them as he used to do by means of articles for the literary journals. Engaged now upon his last solitary journey – and this time he must have guessed where it was leading him – he looked upon the real world, rapidly receding from his view, without regret. Material comforts no longer meant anything to him. Moreover he was no beggar; he still retained his pride. Even in that very bitter winter of 1854/5 the loss of his overcoat was not to be regarded as a hardship.

On 20 January Théophile Gautier and Maxime du Camp were talking together in the editorial office of the *Revue de Paris* when Gérard entered in a threadbare black jacket. It was snowing outside, and a biting north wind swept the streets.

'You are very lightly clad for such cold weather,' Maxime du Camp said to him.

'No,' replied Gérard. 'I am wearing two shirts; there is nothing warmer.'

Théophile objected that he ran the risk of catching pneumonia, and added, 'There are people here who have several overcoats and would be delighted to lend you one for as long as you like.'

'No,' said Gérard again. 'Cold is bracing. The Lapps are never ill.'

Then he began to discourse wildly and only half-quizzically on the sign of Solomon which, he said, the male members of his family bore on the left breast. Finally he drew from his pocket what seemed to be a linen apron string, 'Look what I have just bought,' he said. 'It is the girdle worn by Mme de Maintenon when she played in *Esther* at Saint Cyr.'

It was this same linen cord with which, less than a week later, he was found hanged.

As the three friends went out together into the snow-covered streets, 'Come and have dinner with me, Gérard,'' pleaded Théophile. 'I'll give you a risotto,' and Maxime du Camp added, 'I've a room for you at my house.'

But Gérard showed them a twenty-franc piece which he took from his pocket. 'Thank you,' he said. 'I have my week's supply,' and with that he went off. It was the last they saw of him alive.

On the 22nd Gérard called on Paul Lacroix, generally referred to as the bibliophile Jacob, to confer with him about the proposed list of his complete works, which were to be published by

Dutacq. On that occasion he seemed to be almost quite mad, but at the same time he had never been more full of wit and good humour. Evidently he was experiencing a period of exhilaration, the reaction from which was to reduce him to the lowest level of despair. In company with Georges Bell and Philibert Audebrand he spent the evening of the 24th with Mme Béatrix Person of the Théâtre Historique, sister of the actor Dumaine, who had made something of a name for herself in Dumas's dramas. She was to have played a role in the *Fils Nocturne*, which was never finished. Several scenes were read, and afterwards Gérard appeared to his friends to be unusually cheerful, although there was perhaps a hint of forced gaiety in his merriment, and a note of melancholy in the plaintive airs of the Valois country that he sang to them.

On the way back Gérard stopped to buy a little bread at a baker's and then, bidding his friends goodnight, went off to a tavern in the market to finish an article on the night-life of the city for the *Revue de Paris*. He was working quietly in a corner when a brawl started among the other customers. The police arrived and arrested the culprits. Gérard, too, was questioned.

'What are you doing here?'

'I am thinking.'

To them the reply was a mere impertinence. They searched him, and when they found that he had no money, their suspicions deepened.

'It is true I have no money,' said Gérard, 'but I have paid for the coffee I've just had.'

But the police would not accept his explanation and Gérard spent the night in a cell.

In the morning he sent to a friend, Louis Legrand, an export agent, to come and vouch for him.

'But, my poor Gérard,' said Legrand when he arrived, 'you're frozen.'

'No,' he replied, 'but I'm hungry.'

'Well, we'll go and have lunch. Will you come to my house?'

Gérard refused the invitation on the ground that he had to go in the opposite direction to retrieve his overcoat at the Mont de Piété. He would have sent to Gautier and Houssaye, he said, but they had already come to his rescue on a previous occasion.

'Do you still visit your father?' Legrand asked.

'Yes, I dine with him every Thursday.'

'Why did you pawn your overcoat?'

'It was so fine a week ago that I thought spring had arrived. And then, too, the pawnbrokers look after winter clothes so well! . . .

'I am going to see my father this evening,' Gérard continued.

'Don't worry about me. I can get money from publishers and journals.'

Together they went into a restaurant and Gérard, who until then had appeared quite cheerful, suddenly became depressed. 'I am worried,' he admitted. 'I have ventured on an idea in which I am quite lost. I spend whole hours trying to find myself again. I shall never be able to finish it. Would you believe it, I can scarcely write two lines a day, I am so plunged in gloom. The beginning has already appeared in the *Revue de Paris*. If I don't go on with it, they're going to say again that I am mad.'

On parting after lunch, Legrand persuaded him to accept five francs and then at the last moment, as if urged by a sudden presentiment, he begged Gérard to go home with him or at least to accept something more.

'No,' said Gérard. 'You have lent me a hundred sous; it is more than I need while I am waiting. . . .'

He knew that the end was near and he had no regrets. So long as he remained tied to reality he was doomed to disaster. What was there to stay for? His work was done and the spring of his inspiration dried at the source. The fact that he was destitute no longer concerned him, for he scarcely belonged to the material world any more. He had strayed into a twilight region where all was confusion and from which there seemed to be no escape. He had tried in vain to force the gates of ivory or horn. There was but one way left that would lead him to the star of his aspiration. The steadily darkening shadows of this world had hitherto obscured it, but now he had glimpsed through still deeper shadows the brighter light beyond. The way was clear. He had but to cross the threshold where dream should indeed become reality.

On 24 January he wrote to his aunt, 'My dear aunt, tell your son he does not know that you are the best of mothers and aunts. When I have triumphed over everything, you will have your place in my Olympus, as I have my place in your house. Do not expect me this evening, for the night will be black and white. Gérard Labrunie.'

The same day he called on Méry and, finding him out, he took a sou from his pocket, scratched a cross on it with his pen-knife, and handed it to the servant saying, 'Jean, as soon as your master returns, give him this sou from me.' Méry subsequently interpreted this as a desperate call for help. Certainly Gérard was now completely without resources, but it would seem rather to have been a gesture of prophetic renunciation on his part. The next morning, the 25th, he went to see Asselineau in the Rue de Savoie, and borrowed seven sous to enable him to visit his usual reading-room. 'I don't know what's going to happen to me,' he confided, 'but I am uneasy. For several days now I literally haven't been able to write a line. I'm afraid I shan't be able to produce anything else. . . . I want to try once more today.'

It was his final attempt to finish *Aurélia,* the last fragments of which were found in his pockets after his death. Significantly he was determined to borrow no more than would suffice for his immediate needs. In former days he had been accustomed to borrow from his friends, but always with the prospect of being in a position to repay them very shortly. Now, as scrupulous as ever in these matters, he was unwilling to incur a debt that he would never be able to repay. There were friends who would have been only too willing to advance him money without thought of reimbursement, but Gérard preferred to be free of obligation and modified his requirements accordingly, even to the point of denying himself the bare necessities of life.

In the evening he went to the Théâtre Français and asked for Houssaye. On being told that Houssaye was not there, he left without a word. Later he had something to eat in a tavern in the market and then resumed his wanderings about the frozen streets. It was eighteen degrees below zero. Snow covered the ground and muffled the air so that Paris seemed a deserted city or a city of the dead. At two o'clock in the morning he was stopped and questioned by a police patrol in the Place Bandoyer.

At about three o'clock there was a knock on the door of the cheap lodging-house in the Rue de la Vieille Lanterne. The landlady awoke and turned over in bed. At that hour, and in such weather, she was not going to be disturbed. The knock was not repeated.

On the morning of 26 January 1855, as a grey dawn broke over Paris, the air still heavy with snow, she opened the lower door and stepped out into the alley. With her was a young lad who had found lodging there for the night.

'Look!' he cried out in sudden astonishment, 'What is that gentleman doing down there?'

Seeing the limp figure at the foot of the steps, 'It's a man who has been frozen,' she said.

'No,' replied the other who had gone over to investigate, 'it is a gentleman who has hanged himself.'

The alarm was raised, and very soon a small crowd had assembled round the figure of the man hanging from the grille, grotesquely clad, in those sordid surroundings, in a black coat, grey trousers, patent leather shoes and spats, with a white handkerchief in his breast-pocket and a top-hat on his head. One advised cutting the cord, but another summoned the police. It is said that

F

his right hand was still moving feebly and when the doctor arrived the body was still warm. Prompt action might have saved him, but to what end? He had made his decision. Even in the throes of the last agony he would not have chosen to return.

Artificial respiration was attempted, but it was too late. The body was easily identified, for in the dead man's pockets were found a passport for Constantinople issued on 4 April 1854, in the name of M. Labrunie de Nerval, and one or two receipts. There were also a small notebook, the last few manuscript pages of *Aurélia,* two sous which would have been enough to pay for the night's lodging in the doss-house had it been opened to him, and Asselineau's visiting-card given him during their meeting of the previous day. It was thus Asselineau who was the first to be notified of Gérard's death.

The news soon reached his other friends. Houssaye, one of the first to be informed, hurried to the spot in the Saint Merry quarter, by a curious coincidence the same quarter in which Gérard had been baptized, but by the time he reached the scene the body had already been removed to the morgue. There he met Gautier who, overcome by the sight of his dead friend, grasped the cold hands, sobbing, 'Oh, Gérard, what have you done? Why didn't you come to us yesterday for help?'

Others arrived, among them Nadar, du Camp, Busquet, Asselineau, Michel Levy, Roger de Beauvoir. Many, and especially Roger de Beauvoir, doubted that it was a case of suicide. It seemed incredible to them that Gérard should have been utterly without resources, for all of them would have been only too willing to help him, and they knew that he could have easily obtained advances from various editors. They could not understand his reluctance to live at his friends' expense, to accept further advances on work already in hand or on future work which ultimately he felt himself incapable of executing, or finally to incur debts which there was no prospect of his ever being able to repay.

Even Théophile Gautier, despite his first pitiful exclamation and his subsequent apparent acceptance in two articles of the official verdict of suicide, later firmly believed that Gérard had been set upon and killed. What more likely, in the view of the proponents of this belief, than that Gérard should have been looked upon with suspicion by the sinister types with whom he had associated during his wanderings by night in the most disreputable quarters of Paris? His dress, his general appearance, his conversation and his manner must have seemed utterly incongruous to them. Only two days before his death he had been arrested in company with a number of tavern brawlers, and he alone had been released without question the next morning. Would it not have been natural for them to regard him as in all probability a police informer? The fact that when he was found hanging his hat was still upon his head seemed to indicate an attempt at a coarse jest on the part of his assassins by way of final insult to their victim. Then, too, it had been noted that the toes of the dead man, as he hung from the grille, were just within reach of the ground, and this feature seemed scarcely consonant with a suicide's death. It was suggested that Gérard must have been attacked and killed and then strung up to simulate a hanging, although it would have been far simpler for murderers to have disposed of the body in the river nearby.

It may be remembered that twenty-five years before, the Duc de Bourbon had died in precisely the same way, hanged from a window fastening with his feet just touching the floor, and that it was principally because of this that his wife Sophie had been at first suspected of his murder. On that occasion numerous similar cases of suicide had been cited by the legal and medical expert, Dr Marc, to exonerate her.

In Gérard's case the official verdict of suicide was substantiated by the fact that there were no signs of violence on the body. By reaching out from the bottom step of the flight of steps leading from the street above, he could have attached the cord to the window grille. A stone found nearby might have served him for a final mounting block, to be rolled away as he took the fatal leap. The police, at any rate, were satisfied. When later Houssaye wrote to the commissioner requesting a further enquiry into the matter, he received the following reply : 'Sir, I hasten to inform you that all the enquiries I have made, on receipt of your letter of yesterday's date, have only confirmed me in the opinion that M. Gérard de Nerval committed suicide, as I stated in my report.'

One fact alone remained unexplained, that three hours had elapsed between the time that Gérard knocked at the door of the lodging-house and the time that he was hanged. What had he done during the interval? It is scarcely to be imagined that he would have spent three hours pondering in the bitter cold of that freezing January night before making his fatal decision. Had he slept? Thinly clad as he was, with only his two cotton shirts and two flannel vests besides his threadbare jacket to protect him from the cold, had he lain down to sleep the probability is that he would never have awakened. Is it not possible that the clue to the solution is provided by a recollection of the curious method of sleeping that Gérard adopted when travelling by diligence with Gautier in 1836? It will be re-called that then he would attach a scarf by the two ends to the roof of the vehicle so as to form a sort of noose into which he would insert his head preparatory to sleeping, and that Théophile was surprised that he was not 'well and truly strangled'. Was his death perhaps after all an accident?

Finding himself shut out and disappointed of his last hope of shelter for the night, tired out with walking and desperately in need of sleep yet sensibly hesitating to risk freezing to death by lying down in an open doorway, might he not have resolved to snatch a little sleep while standing? A stone lying near the foot of the steps would have offered a convenient perch to keep his thin and all too permeable shoes out of the snow, while the grille above perhaps reminded him of that old habit of his early travelling days. It may be that, drawing the linen cord from his pocket, he tied it to the grille and passed his head through the noose, as then. Thus settled he could be sure of not sleeping too long. It may be that, in this strange but to him familiar attitude, he confidently resigned himself to rest, although this time, in Théo's words, he was not to be 'spared the penalty of hanging himself'. A movement in his sleep, or perhaps on waking, could have rolled the stone from under him and left him helplessly suspended.

Whether he actually died by accident or whether by design must remain a matter of conjecture. Certainly the question of suicide had frequently occupied his thoughts, and on several occasions, as we have seen, he had been strongly tempted to put an end to his life, although something had always help him back. He had once said to Houssaye : 'When I kill myself, it will not be with a pistol.'

If then, he had so many times resisted the temptation to destroy himself, what, we may ask, could have driven him to succumb to it in the end? 'Suicide', we are told in *Emilie*, 'is nothing but the supreme act of egoism, and that is why it is stigmatized among men.' It is generally considered that egoism and altruism are diametrically opposed and that the one characteristic of necessity excludes the other. But Gérard was, as we have seen, compact of opposites. We know, from the opinions expressed by his friends and acquaintances, from his letters and from his life, that he was modest and unassuming, courteous, kind-hearted, generous, and scrupulously honest. His egoism, if such it can be termed, derived solely from his mysticism, and resolved itself into the need to isolate himself from the crowd in order to penetrate the mysteries of the 'outer world', as he termed it. At the same time he was naturally of a sociable disposition and, shy as he was, he delighted in company. Those last days of extreme poverty and distress must have been doubly hard for him to endure, lacking the society of his friends, and indeed both Delvau and Houssaye concurred in suggesting that it was loneliness that finally drove him to despair.

Like Cowper, he was 'a stricken deer that left the herd', for he would not inflict his sufferings on his friends. Only among strangers who knew nothing of his background could he feel at ease for a little, and it was perhaps as much for the sense of companionship they afforded as for documentary purposes in connection with his proposed work on the night life of Paris that he retreated into the more disreputable quarters of the city where he was not recognized and where even the signs of madness might be taken for mere eccentricity.

The story of *Emilie,* although it originated with Gérard, was in execution largely, perhaps entirely the work of Maquet, his frequent collaborator. A more authentic, as well as a more pertinent statement of Gérard's own view of suicide than that quoted above from *Emilie* is to be found in *Aurélia,* where he says 'despair and suicide are the results of certain situations fatal for one who has not faith in immortality, with all its griefs and joys.' There can be little doubt that this faith was in fact the invisible power that had previously prevented him from killing himself. The ecstatic and triumphant ending of *Aurélia* with its firm conviction of the immortality of the spirit would seem immediately to preclude the possibility of his succumbing to such an ultimate despair. But in the wider context the alternating elation and depression that was so typical of the dialectic of his mental condition made it almost inevitable that at some point there would be a plunge into the deepest gloom, a third descent into hell, from which this time there would be no return.

How far he was already involved in this descent may be gauged from the sardonic lines (rhymed in the original) addressed in a letter to the Princesse de Solms and from the sonnet that followed.

> I am an idle journalist living from hand to mouth,
> Who make my dinner of a slice of bread.
> Old before my time and filled with bitter rancour,
> Suspicious as a rat, deceived by too many people,
> Having no belief in sincere friendships,
> I have purposely put an end to the noble sentiments
> That persuaded you, Madam, to relieve the torments
> Of a soul abandoned to the regions of misery. . . .
> My pen is frozen in the dark days of winter;
> With no fire in my hovel, no panes in my windows,
> I am going to find a *pad* in heaven or hell,
> And I have at last buttoned myself up for the other world.
> I have written my epitaph and take the liberty
> Of dedicating it to you in a foolish sonnet

Which now jets up from the bottom of an empty brain . . .
Cuckoo-clock stopped by the cold :
Misery has undermined my thoughts.

Sonnet

Sometimes he lived as gay as a lark,
By turns amorous, tender, carefree,
Sometimes like a sad lover in dark reverie.
One day at his door he heard a knock.

It was Death ! And he asked her only to wait
Till his final sonnet's last line should be filled,
Then quietly went to stretch himself out
In the coffin where his body shivered with cold.

He was often lazy, so it is said,
Too often the ink in his ink-well dried.
Though he sought to know all, he knew nothing in sum.

When the moment came that, tired of life,
One winter's evening his soul made off,
He went away saying : Why did I come?

Unable to write, haunted by the spectre of his madness, too
poor to enjoy the company of his friends, whose pity and sympathy
he shunned, he had little enough to live for, and while he still
lived, he was separated from his ideal love. Death alone offered
release. For a long time now he had been but a simulacrum of
himself. His mistake had been to imagine that he could exist
upon another plane while still bound to the material world by
the body with all its implacable demands. Cast that aside and he
would be free to cross the threshold into that other world which
was his true reality and where the Aurélia of his dreams, at once
mother, bride and goddess, waited to welcome him. To die, then,
would be an act of triumph, not surrender.

Dr Labrunie, then in his seventy-ninth year, received the news
of his son's death with the equanimity of an old man nearing his
end, to whom nothing in life was any longer very important, 'Ah,'
he said to Auguste Chatillon who broke the news to him, 'the young
man is dead ! The poor boy ! I am very sorry. He was a good
fellow. Poor young man ! He came to see me now and then, at
intervals. Tell me, sir, what is to happen about the funeral?' Chatillon assured him that his son's friends were taking care of every-

thing. 'Well,' he said with evident relief, "that's all for the best, for at my age and with my health such as it is, it would be difficult for me to discharge the duty. Ah! the poor young man!'

The body had been claimed by the Society of Men of Letters and, at Houssaye's instigation, the management of the Théâtre Français undertook to defray the funeral expenses. The following letter from Dr Blanche to the archbishop of Paris was enough to ensure that the suicide would not be deprived of a Christian burial:

M. Labrunie (Gérard de Nerval), aged forty-five years, born in Paris, author, was overcome several times during the latter years by an access of mental alienation, for which my father and I attended him. Towards the end, on 12 October 1853, M. Gérard de Nerval was brought to me in a state of violent delirium; after some months of treatment, he made a convalescent journey into Germany; shortly after his return, he fell ill again and, on 8 August, 1854, he was once more entrusted to my care. This last crisis was less prolonged and on 19 October, at his entreaty, I handed him over to the care of his aunt, Mme Labrunie, who, having been warned by me that M. Gérard still had need of some supervision, undertook to receive him and to look after him. In fact, M. Gérard de Nerval was not so ill as to justify his being confined against his will in a lunatic asylum, but, in my view, for a long time he had not been sane. Believing that he still had the the same vigour of imagination and the same aptitude for work, he expected to be able to live, as before, on the proceeds from his works; he worked more than ever, but were his hopes deceived? His independent nature and his pride were opposed to his receiving anything, even from the best-proved friendships. It was under the influence of these moral causes that his reason wandered more and more; it was above all because he saw his madness face to face. I do not hesitate to declare to you, my lord, that it was certainly in an access of madness that M. Gérard de Nerval put an end to his life.

Any final scruples were effectually dispelled by the pronouncement of the ecclesiastic officiating at the service in Notre Dame on 30 January 1855; 'Did anyone see this unfortunate man hang himself? No, nobody. It is our duty therefore to suppose that he was the victim of a crime.'

More than three hundred people, for the most part poets, writers and artists, attended the obsequies and followed the coffin to the cemetery of Père Lachaise. Among his closest friends who accompanied Gérard's remains to the graveside, Théophile Gautier was conspicuous by the yellow scarf he wore wound round his head because of an abscess from which he was suffering. Victor Hugo alone was absent, exiled in Jersey. Alexandre Dumas wrote to him on the eve of the funeral: 'My very dear and very great, you know that our poor Gérard has committed suicide or else been murdered. He is to be buried tomorrow. Arsène Houssaye is in charge of all the details of the cortège. This is what I wrote to him yesterday: "My dear Houssaye, if Victor Hugo had been in Paris, he would have done our dear Gérard the honour of carrying one corner of the pall. I think that, in the absence of our great poet, it is our duty to leave Hugo's place vacant and to have only three or five bearers. I make the suggestion; it is for you to decide. Yours, Al. Dumas." Houssaye has replied: "Yes, till Thursday morning, Arsène Houssaye." You see that I lose no opportunity of protesting against your absence. Tomorrow, then, you will be among us.' Francis Wey pronounced a funeral oration at the grave-side, and the coffin was lowered into the earth.

Six weeks later Dr Labrunie authorized Gautier and Houssaye to erect a plain granite column over the tomb. But the site acquired by M. Godefroy of the Society of Men of Letters the day before the funeral, had not been acquired in perpetuity. The amount subscribed had been sufficient only for a concession of ten years, and when, in March 1867, no further subscription having been raised, the body was exhumed, Gautier and Houssaye obtained the permanent concession of a new site in another part of the cemetery.

Houssaye in his *Confessions* has recorded how he and Théophile witnessed the exhumation and reburial. 'The poor skeleton was in pieces, Death having accomplished her work rapidly. Horrible spectacle: the head which had exhibited virile beauty was no longer represented even by a simple skull. Thousands of worms hung suspended from it in bunches and were almost ossified there. It was a veritable labour to disengage them: we were no longer breathing.'

Above the new tomb was erected a white marble column supporting a veiled urn. It bore merely the words, 'To Gérard de Nerval', and, in smaller letters on the base, 'His friend Arsène Houssaye'. Thus at last the poor fragmentary remains of the once charming and spiritual Gérard found a companionable resting-place between the tombs of Balzac, Casimir Delavigne and Charles Nodier.

16

The Last Works

For more than seventy years after his death Gérard de Nerval's genius remained unrecognized. Disregarded by the critics in general, he was at most granted a superficial mention as a minor romantic, author of *Sylvie*, with an appealing vein of pastoral simplicity. *Aurélia* and the later poems were overlooked as the obscure productions of a disordered mind. In an age of realism it was perhaps natural that he should have been dismissed as a mere escapist, a denizen of (in Sainte-Beuve's phrase, which he himself adopted) 'the ivory tower', a frail, neurotic figure defeated by life, lacking the stature or the stamina to survive the struggle. It is true that, conditioned by his early upbringing under almost exclusively feminine influences, he developed a sensibility ill-designed to prepare him for the harsher aspects of life, but his independence of spirit would not allow him tamely to submit to his destiny. 'Truly,' he wrote in *Paradoxe et Verité*, 'the world in which we live is a gambling-house and a bad place, and I am ashamed to think that God sees me in it.' Like Novalis before him, he sought to enrich life by discovering within himself the secret of the universe. Dream and vision led him into a mystical world of fantastic correspondences, and so eventually to madness where he became the victim of his own myth. It was the penalty of his promethean revolt, a revolt illustrated by another passage from *Paradoxe et Verité* : 'I do not ask God to change anything in the way of events, but to change me in relation to things; to allow me the power . . . to direct my eternal dream instead of submitting to it.' Identifying himself as one of the descendants of Cain, sons of the fire, in revolt against Death and Time, he tentatively expresses his protest, largely by implication, in the *Filles du Feu*.

The book is of very uneven quality. It consists of the dedication to Alexandre Dumas, seven stories – *Angélique*, *Sylvie* (followed by the *Chansons et Légendes du Valois*), *Jemmy*, *Octavie*, *Isis*, *Corilla*, *Emilie* – and the twelve sonnets comprising *Les Chimères*, somewhat hastily and arbitrarily collected together to form a volume. Of the stories the least authentic are *Jemmy*, which is simply a translation of a German story by Charles Sealsfield, and *Emilie*, which is largely the work of Auguste Maquet. Slight as it is, *Corilla,* a dramatic interlude originally written for Jenny Colon in 1839, is of interest as illustrating the continuity of Gérard's favourite themes and obsessions, in particular that of the 'double'. The remaining four stories fall naturally into two pairs. In *Octavie* and *Isis* the scene is Italy, with the hidden fire of Vesuvius in the background to remind us of the myth. That of *Angélique* and *Sylvie* is the Ile de France.

Octavie is the story of his meetings with a young English girl[1] some time during his visits to Italy. Octavie herself is a creation of fantasy, a composite figure originally suggested by a chance encounter on the ship that took him to Marseilles in 1834. Once more the theme of resemblances is exploited, and there are parallels with the story of *Sylvie*. Both narratives begin in the theatre where the figure of Aurélia appears every evening strangely etherealized by the artificial stage lighting. By contrast both Sylvie and Octavie, biting with her ivory teeth into the bitter rind of the lemon of experience,[2] represent the return to reality. Both stories conclude with the same observation, 'perhaps there lay true happiness', that is to say, in reality rather than in fantasy. It is this conflict between the real and the ideal that constitutes the drama of the stories and indeed of his whole life, for however little trust one can put in the factual details of the narration, there is not the slightest doubt that it provides a true spiritual autobiography. From the transient vision of Adrienne in his youth Gérard had constructed an ideal which he was doomed to suffer disillusionment in not encountering in real life. It was this, above all, aggravated by the fact that all the seeming incarnations of the ideal – Adrienne, Sophie, Jenny – were apparently destined, like his mother, to die young, that drove him more and more to seek reality in the other world of dream. It may truly be said that Nerval possessed in a high degree what Miguel de Unamuno has called 'the tragic sense of life which carries with it an entire conception of life itself and of the universe, a whole philosophy more or less formulated, more or less conscious.' Unamuno describes it as follows : 'Living is one thing, knowing is another, and there is perhaps such an opposition between them that we may say everything vital is not merely irrational but anti-rational, and everything rational is antivital. And this is the basis of the tragic sense of life.' Among others, he cites, as typical

---

[1] The meeting referred to on pp 65–66.

[2] *Sylvie* : 'The illusions fall away like the peel of a fruit, and the fruit itself is experience. Its taste is bitter; yet it has a tartness which invigorates one.'

examples of those who possess this tragic sense of life, Marcus Aurelius, Saint Augustine, Pascal, Rousseau, Leopardi, Amiel, and Kierkegaard, 'men loaded with wisdom rather than learning'. Certainly Nerval deserves a place amongst this company of tormented and illustrious spirits.

Octavie, though a moving work tinged with an inescapable melancholy, is in the final analysis imperfect and unsatisfying. But as providing a transitional link between *Sylvie* and *Aurélia* and, together with its pendant *Isis,* a key to the personal significance of certain features of the Nervalian mythology, it is of paramount importance.

In *Isis,* Gérard offers a succinct exposition of the syncretism that he had first begun to develop during his eastern journey. The divinity here celebrated, the queen of heaven, 'of varied attributes and changing appearance', is in fact the eternal Mother, Isis or the Holy Virgin; 'the same sign of the Zodiac is consecrated to them, the moon is beneath their feet; the same halo encircles their heads.' Remembering how Delphine appeared at Senlis with an aureole about her head, standing on a hemisphere representing a burnt-out star, and Adrienne similarly at Châalis; Jenny, too, haloed by the spotlight, on the lit circle of the stage, and finally Aurélia 'with the features of a divinity', beneath whose feet turned a wheel; one can follow the successive stages by which, in a syncretism parallel to the religious, the varying aspects of the ideal are finally unified in the one mediating figure – mother-bride-divinity-Isis-the Virgin Mary.

Just as in *Octavie* Gérard may be seen to be engaged in reconstructing a mythical life for himself outside time, of which the reality is only a pale reflection, so in *Angélique* he begins to rediscover the remote mythical past of his earliest days in the Valois country.

To a great extent it was this rediscovery that inspired the exquisite masterpiece *Sylvie.* Short as it is, simple and artless as it may appear superficially, it gave him more trouble than any of his other writings, and he was occupied on it for eighteen months, constantly revising, correcting, polishing. This is not to be wondered at, for it is a work of unique originality, and in it Gérard attains the perfection of his art.

In the dedicatory introduction to the *Filles du Feu* addressed to Dumas, he speaks of the sonnet, 'El Desdichado', as being written in a mood of what he terms 'supernaturalist reverie'. *Sylvie,* conceived in the same way, is yet ordered throughout by a clear and purposeful intellect, with its subtly manipulated counterpoint of the three principal themes – the romantic, the religious, and the real, personified in the actress, the nun, and the simple village girl, Aurélia, Adrienne, and Sylvie – its delicate modulations of key, and its dominating atmosphere of mysterious enchantment finally resolving itself into a nostalgic melancholy. Gérard's actual experience of what he described as 'the spilling-over of dream into real life' has here invaded his writing, providing him with a technique that enables him to invest his narrative with a depth of meaning which is the result of suggestion rather than explicit statement. The interrelation of three separate planes of existence by alternating actuality, reverie and dream is so skilfully managed that the whole emerges as a perfectly balanced unity, a crystal drop within the mirroring depths of which childhood love is perpetuated. It was evidently this recapture of lost time that so commanded Proust's admiration.

Nerval achieves it in part also by the evocative power of his writing. Speaking of Heine's poetry, he remarked that 'the words do not describe objects, they evoke them', and this applies equally well to his own work. Yet there is nothing blurred or indistinct about it. On the contrary there is a clarity of vision matched by a limpidity of style that, despite his predilection for the misty landscapes of the Valois, invests the scene with something of the exact definition of paintings of the Dutch school which he so much admired. There is no attempt at elaborate description. It is rather with the affective atmosphere that he is concerned. In conformity with the constant interplay of reverie and reality, the one merging into the other, there is a notable emphasis on fluid and changing elements – the effects of light, the movement of trees in the wind, reflections in the still surface of the ponds or the flowing water of the streams, sounds of hunting horns, girls' voices, bird song, and the colours and scents of innumerable flowers, all of which have their symbolic value.

Just as *Sylvie* represents his revolt against time, so *Aurélia* represents his revolt against death. These were the two enemies, in order to overcome which he dedicated himself to the discovery of a reality beyond that of everyday existence. The key to this reality, he believed, lay in dream. He believed, with Baudelaire, that 'the faculty of dreaming is a divine and mysterious faculty; for it is by dream that man communicates with the shadowy world by which he is surrounded.' Thus he constructed for himself a world of essences superior to the world of appearances. It was to this world of essences that his ideal love belonged in an eternal present, and it was only in the familiar world of appearances that she seemed to be presented under different guises. To be united with her immortal essence in that world of true reality was the object of his endeavour. For this it was necessary, in Rimbaud's words, 'to be a seer, to make oneself a seer . . . by an infinite, prolonged and reasoned derangement of all the senses', involving 'love, suffering and madness'. Whether by poetry or dream or esoteric practices, this attempt to 'reach the unknown' was a blasphemy for which he felt himself to be accursed. So in *Aurélia* he wrote, 'I was cursed perhaps for having wanted to penetrate a fearful mystery, and so having offended against the divine law; I must expect only anger and contempt for ever! The angry shadows fled, uttering wild cries and tracing ominous circles in the air, like birds at the approach of a storm.' Aurélia is lost and the only way of winning her back is by the way of repentance; hence the agonized self-accusations of the second part of the book and the recognition for the need for expiation. Repentance however is not sufficient in itself, and there arises the need for an intercessor. Finally it is Aurélia herself who becomes for him the natural and supreme mediatress, and it is in her company that in a final vision he rides triumphantly to his salvation. Death is conquered and immortality is assured. 'I am happy in the convictions I have acquired,' he concludes, 'and I compare this series of ordeals I have endured with what for the Ancients represented the idea of a descent into Hell.'

Owing to the destruction of all Dr Blanche's papers in a fire, the true nature of Gérard's mental illness remains a matter of inference and conjecture. At that time the study of mental disorders was in its infancy, and such terms as 'paranoia' and 'manic-depressive' were introduced only much later. From a letter to his father dated 7 October 1853 it would appear that Dr Blanche's treatment was of the mildest, confined largely to baths, purgative pills and soothing drinks but, as Gérard himself confessed, it was rather his sympathy and understanding that exercised such a beneficial effect on his patient. Dr Blanche emerges as a man of infinite patience and understanding. Difficult as his patient must have been, he had a very real friendship for him and never ceased to encourage him in his writing. It will be remembered that it was Blanche who encouraged him to write down his impressions of his illness, an undertaking that resulted in *Aurélia*. That the final work transcends the original intention was due to the extraordinary power of Gérard's symbolic vision which raises the account of a purely individual personal experience to the level of a universal myth of man's struggle against his destiny.

All these later prose works are closely related to the handful of poems written between 1843 and 1854, twelve sonnets in as many years, collected under the title *Les Chimères*, chimeras, fantasies which represent the summit of Gérard de Nerval's achievement. Of his own poetry he wrote, 'My first poems were inspired by the enthusiasm of youth, the next by love, the last by despair. The muse invaded my heart like a goddess with golden words; she escaped from it like a pythoness uttering cries of grief.'

Certainly there is nothing in the earlier poems to foreshadow the depth and mastery of these sonnets. The most accomplished of the early works, the *Odelettes,* are in the main slight and artificial. Nevertheless one or two of these are of particular interest as introducing typically Nervalian themes; notably 'Fantaisie' with its symbol of the castle, a reminiscence of the château of Mortefontaine and its emphasis on the idea of a pre-existence, and 'Le Point Noir' with its suggestion of the 'Black sun of Melancholy', an image derived originally from Dürer's engraving of the angel of melancholy, which had a peculiar fascination for Nerval.

Such recurrent thoughts and images may be traced throughout the prose works too, culminating in the sonnets. The famous opening of 'El Desdichado', for instance, is anticipated in the fragment of the uncompleted *Roman Tragique* quoted in the introduction to the *Filles du Feu* : 'the unrecognized prince, the mysterious lover, the disinherited, the exile from joy, the fine man of darkness'. In the same sonnet the vine and the rose and the siren recall *Octavie,* as do also the volcano of 'Myrtho' and the bitter lemons of 'Delfica'. This continuity and development of thought is reflected again in the embodiment of such familiar themes as that of revolt in 'Anteros', of pythagoreanism in 'Delfica' and 'Vers Dorés', of syncretism in 'Artemis', 'Horus' and 'Le Christ aux Oliviers'.

Indeed it is because the whole of Nerval's experience is condensed within the brief, densely packed space of these sonnets that a close study of his other works is necessary to elucidate much of the elaborate and sometimes obscure symbolism. Yet, as he wrote to Dumas, 'they are hardly more obscure than Hegel's metaphysic or Swedenborg's *Memorabilia* and would lose some of their charm in being explained, if that were possible.' Their difficulty arises from their extraordinary compactness, to which the absence of all unnecessary transitional links contributes. They are evocative and deeply emotional; yet the expression is perfectly controlled in the strictest of traditional forms. They have the direct appeal of pure poetry, attaining their effect by a cumulative series of overtones, expanding inexhaustibly in the mind like the rings on the surface of a pool when a stone is dropped into it. Although intensely personal in origin, they have the range and power of universal myth and invite endless interpretations. It was exactly this faculty of transcending his own sufferings and giving a universal meaning to his own individual experience that was the core of Gérard de Nerval's genius.

Chronology

1807	Marriage of Etienne Labrunie to Marie Antoinette Marguerite Laurent.
1808	(22 May) Gérard Labrunie born in Paris at 96 Rue Saint-Martin.
	(5 November) Marguerite (Jenny) Colon born at Boulogne.
1810	(29 November) Death of Gérard's mother in Silesia.
1814	Gérard's father, Etienne Labrunie, returns to Paris, 72 Rue Saint-Martin.
1820	Gérard enters the Lycée Charlemagne in Paris, where Théophile Gautier is his fellow-pupil.
	(30 May) Death of his uncle Antoine Boucher at Mortefontaine.
1826	Death of his aunt Eugénie.
1828	Publication of Gérard's translation of Goethe's *Faust*. First meeting with Victor Hugo and his circle.
1830	The battle of *Hernani*.
1831	First dramatic pieces accepted.
1832	Gérard, student of medicine, joins Jehan Duseigneur's group of artists and writers.
1834	He inherits thirty thousand francs on the death of his grandfather.
	Journey to Italy.
1835	Joins Rogier, Gautier, Esquiros, etc, in the Rue du Doyenné. Foundation of the *Monde Dramatique*.

1836	Failure of the *Monde Dramatique*. Gérard and Théo visit Belgium.
1837	Première of *Piquillo*.
1838	Jenny Colon marries Leplus. Gérard's first journey to Germany, in company with Dumas.
1839	*Léo Burckart* produced at the Porte Saint-Martin. Journey to Austria.
1840	Journey to Belgium. *Piquillo* produced in Brussels. Death of Sophie Dawes, baroness de Feuchères.
1841	(23 February) First mental crisis. (21 March) Relapse. Gérard under the care of Dr Esprit Blanche at Montmartre.
1842	(5 June) Death of Jenny Colon. Gérard leaves for the Orient towards the end of December.
1843	Travels in the Near East. Returns in December.
1844	Travels with Houssaye in Belgium and Holland.
1845	Visits London for eight days in August.
1846	Peregrinations in the Valois.
1848	Translation of Heine's poems appears in the *Revue des Deux Mondes*.
1849	(April) Fresh attack of Gérard's mental illness. In care of Dr Ley and Dr Aussandon. (May–June) Visits London.
1850	(May) Again under the care of Dr Aussandon. (August–September) Travels in Germany.
1851	Publication of the *Voyage en Orient*. (24 September) A fall induces another mental crisis. With Dr Emile Blanche at Passy.
1852	(January–February) Treated in the Maison Dubois. (May) Travels in Holland. August in the Valois. (November) Publication of *Les Illuminés*.

1853   (February–March) Again in the Maison Dubois.

(15 August) Publication of *Sylvie* in the *Revue des Deux Mondes*.

(25 August) Fresh attack of mental illness. With Dr Blanche at Passy.

1854   Publication of *Les Filles du Feu and Les Chimères*.

(27 May) Gérard leaves for Germany.

(August–October) Again under the care of Dr Blanche.

1855   (26 January) Gérard found hanged in the Rue de a Vieille Lanterne.

Selected Bibliography

PRINCIPAL WORKS OF GÉRARD DE NERVAL

PROSE

1832   *La Main enchantée*

1839   *Corilla*

1841   *Les Amours de Vienne*

1842   *Chansons et Legendes de Valois*
       Octavie

1851   *Voyage en Orient*

1852   *Les Nuits d'Octobre*

1852   *Les Illuminés*
       Lorely: Souvenirs d'Allemagne

1853   *Petits Châteaux de Bohème*
       Sylvie

1854   *Promenades et Souvenirs*
       La Pandora
       Les Filles du Feu

1855   *Aurélia*

POETRY

1828   Translation of Goethe's *Faust* in prose and verse

1844   *Le Christ aux Oliviers*

1845   *Delfica. Vers Dorés*

1853   *El Desdichado*

1854   *Myrtho. Horus. Anteros. Artemis*

PLAYS

1839 *Léo Burckart*

COLLECTED WORKS

1952 Vol. I. Bibliothèque de la Pléiade

1958 Vol. II. Bibliothèque de la Pléiade

1958 2 Vols. Classiques Garnier

TRANSLATIONS

1958 Geoffrey Wagner, *Selected Writings* (Peter Owen)

1972 Norman Glass, *Journey to the Orient* (Peter Owen)

SHORT LIST OF WORKS ON GÉRARD DE NERVAL AND HIS WRITINGS

1914 Aristide Marie, *Gérard de Nerval* (Hachette)

1926 Pierre Audiat, *L'Aurélia de Gérard de Nerval* (Champion)

1945 Albert Beguin, *Gérard de Nerval* (Corti)

1946 Camille Ducray, *Gérard de Nerval* (Tallandier)

1948 L. H. Sebillotte, *Le Secret de Gérard de Nerval* (Corti)

1949 Jeanine Moulin, *Les Chimères de Gérard de Nerval* (Droz)

1950 Jean Richer, *Gérard de Nerval* (Seghers)

1953 Francis Carco, *Gérard de Nerval* (Michel)

1956 Léon Cellier, *Gérard de Nerval* (Hatier)

1956 Jean Gaulmier, *Gérard de Nerval et les 'Filles du Feu'* (Nizet)

1963 Marie de Vivier, *Gérard de Nerval* (La Palatine)

1964 Raymond Jean, *Nerval par lui-même* (Ed. du Seuil)

1965 Eduard Peyrouzet, *Gérard de Nerval Inconnu* (Corti)

1966   Pierre Moreau, *Sylvie et ses sources* (Soc. d'Ed. d'Enseignement Supérieur)

1968   Kurt Schärer, *Thématique de Nerval* (Lettres Modernes. Minard)

1972   André Lebois, *Fabuleux Nerval* (Denoël)

Printed in Dunstable, United Kingdom

85047121R00107